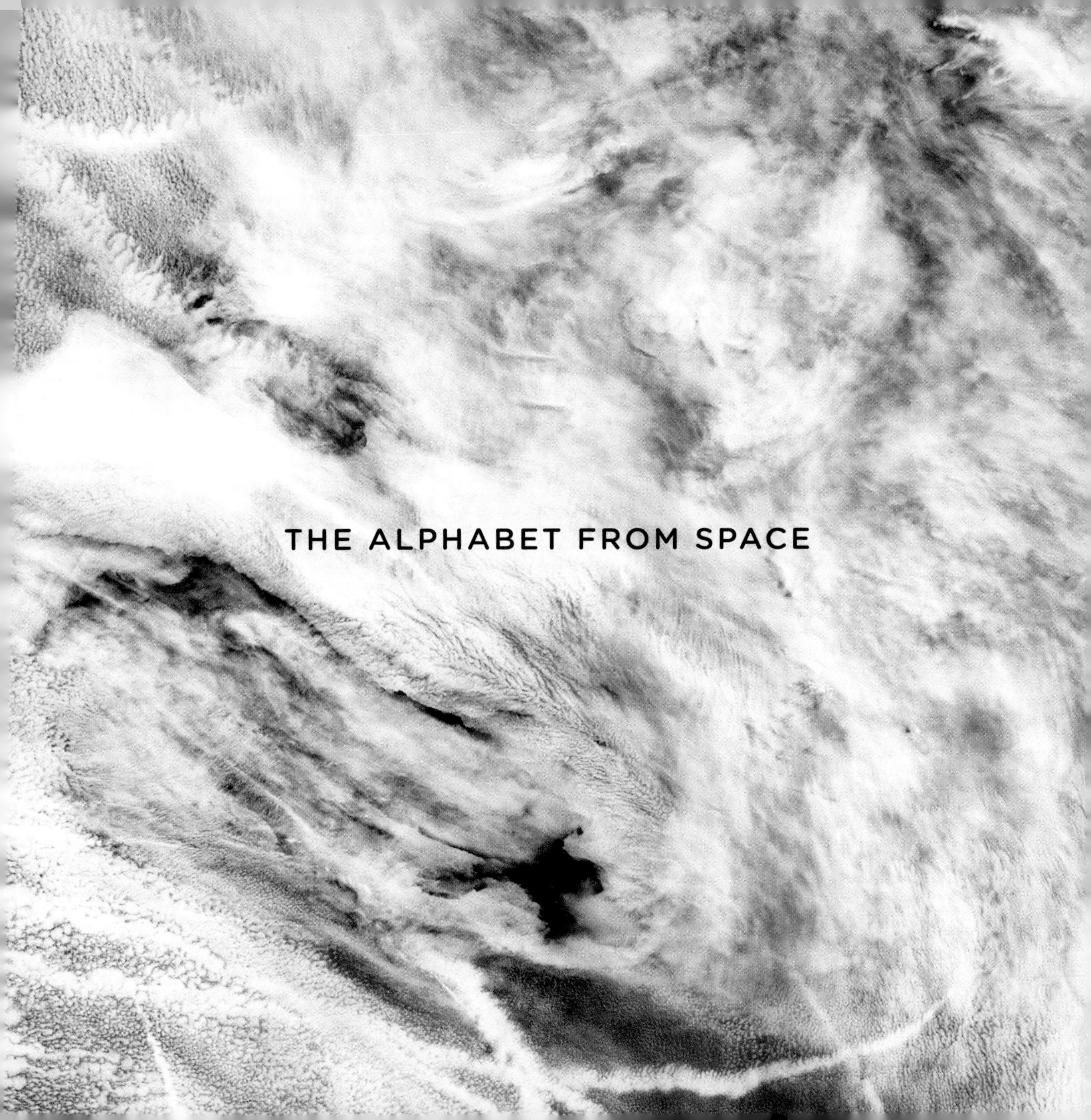

THE ALPHABET FROM SPACE

For my dear Calvin and all the other curious children (and their parents) in the world. Never stop wondering. Never stop asking questions.

First published in Great Britain in 2016 by

Quercus Editions Ltd
Carmelite House
50 Victoria Embankment
London EC4Y 0DZ
An Hachette UK company

A CIP catalogue record for this book is available from the British Library

HB ISBN 978 1 78648 127 6

Ebook ISBN 978 1 78648 129 0

10 9 8 7 6 5 4 3 2 1

Designed and illustrated by Sarah Greeno
sarahgreeno.com
limitededitiondesign.co.uk

A special thank you to Jesse Allen for his help in processing the satellite imagery.

Printed and bound in Italy by L.E.G.O S.p.A

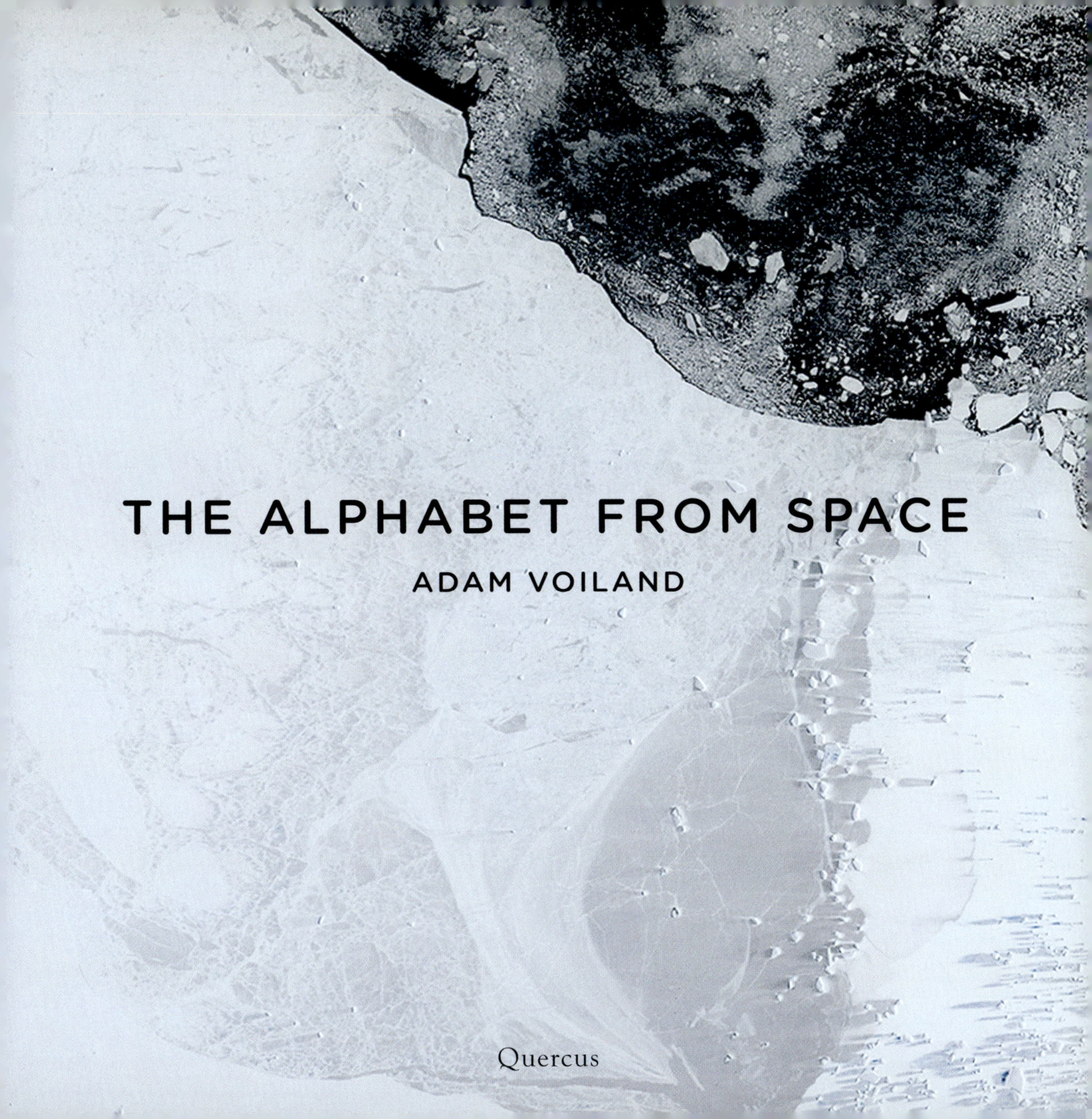

THE ALPHABET FROM SPACE

ADAM VOILAND

Quercus

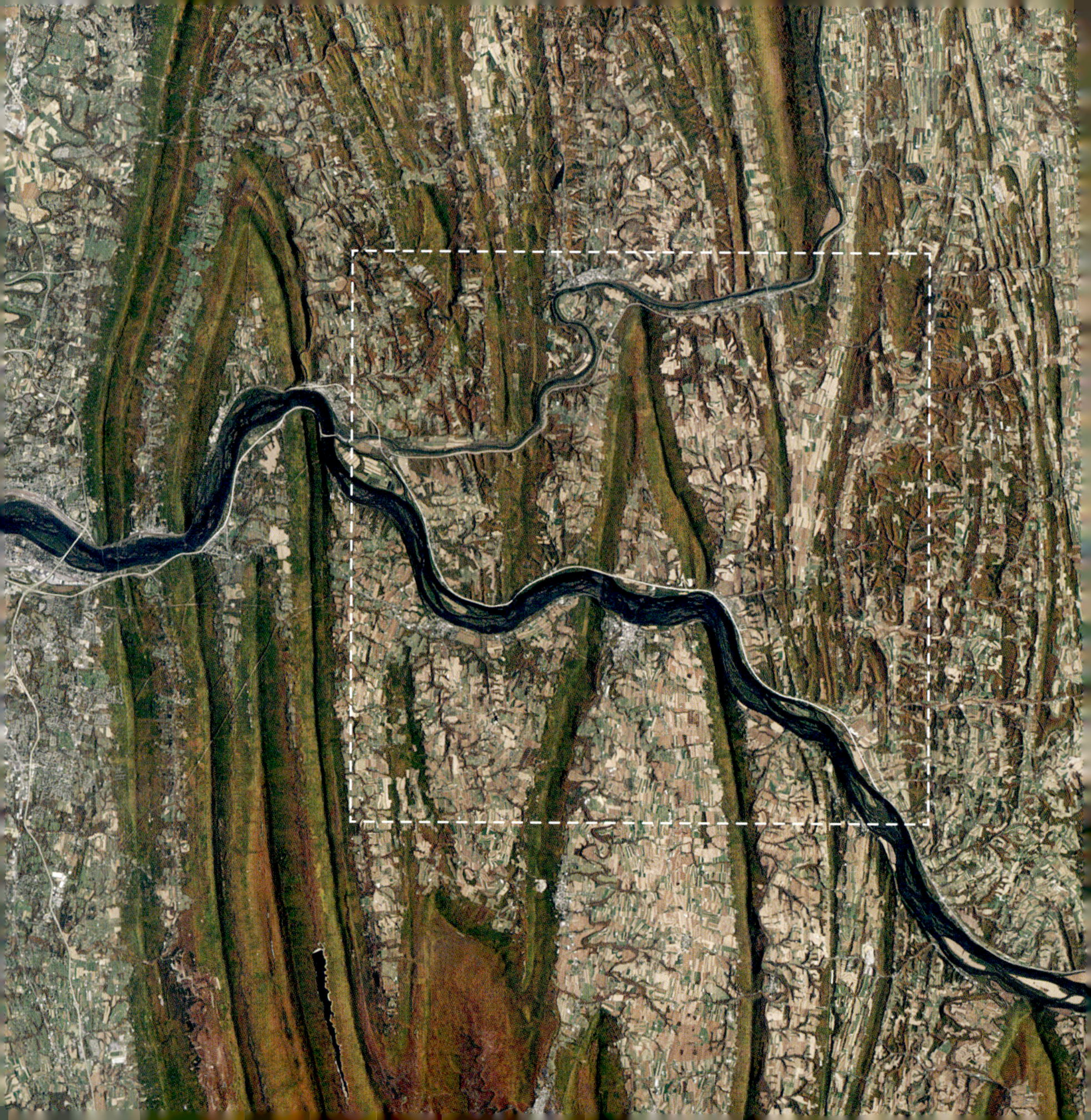

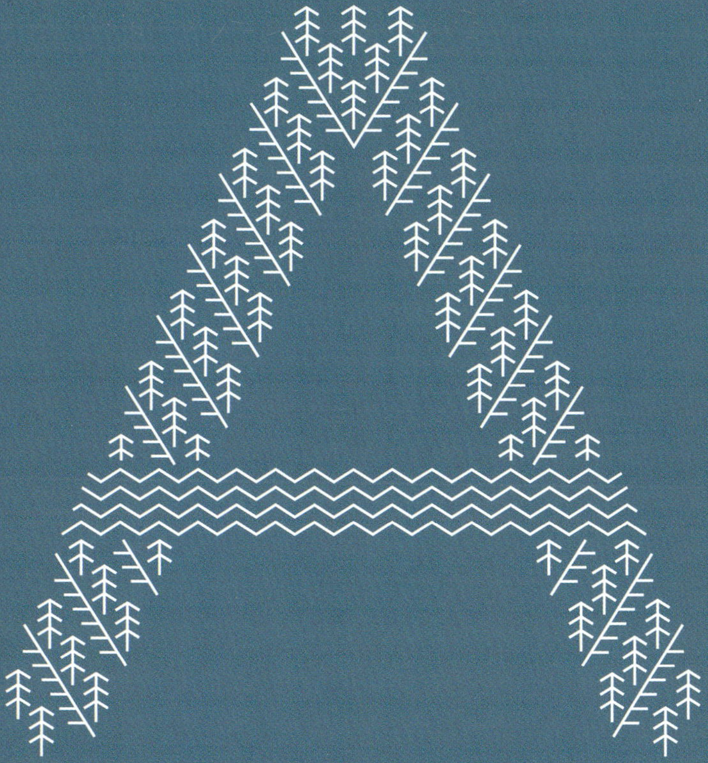

Aloha, **A**! What begins with A? Antarctica, Azerbaijan, **algal blooms** and **alluvial fans**. Astronauts appreciating awe-inspiring views of Earth from above. And these ancient Appalachian ridges in America crossed by an azure river in autumn!

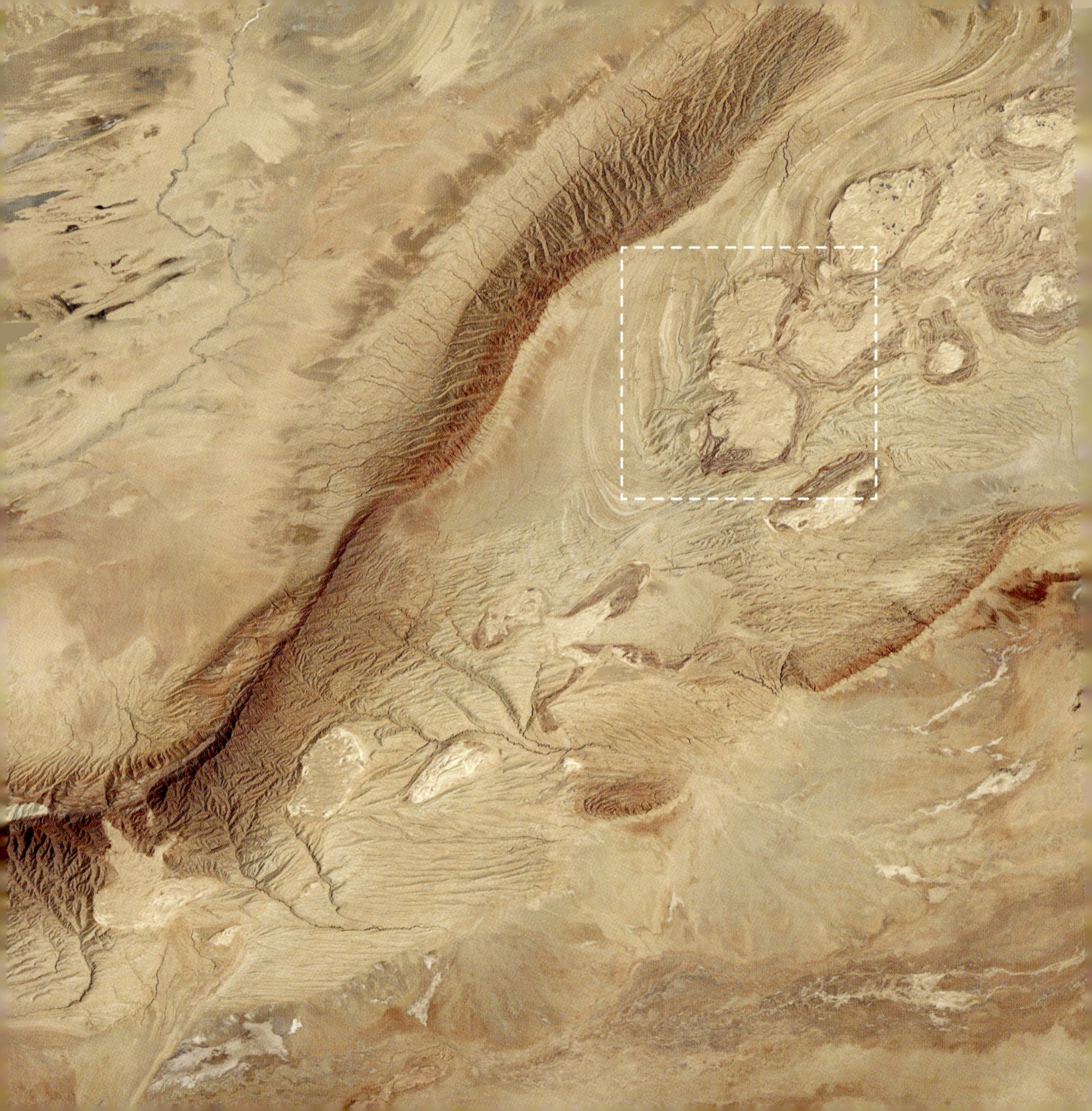

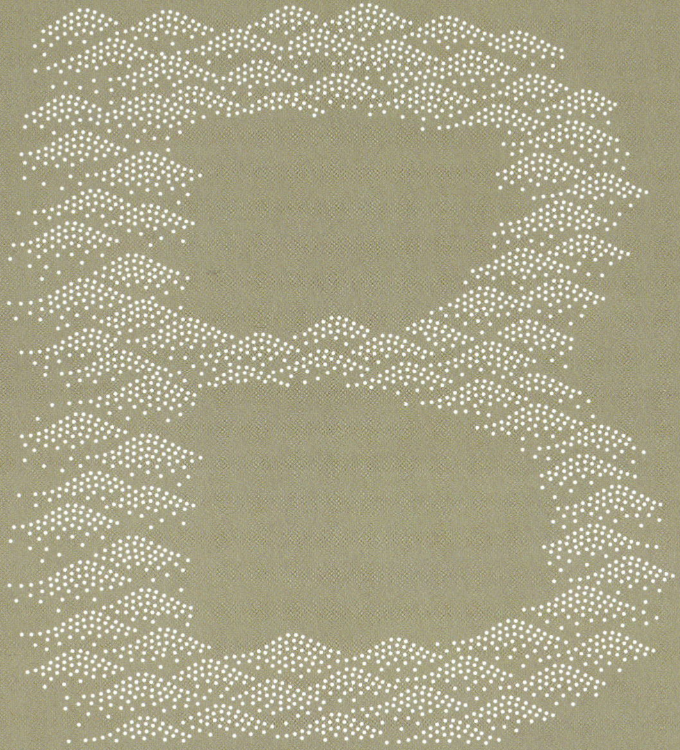

Bonjour, **B**. Barcelona and Beijing begin with B. Actually, everything did, with a **Big Bang** billions of years ago. The itsy-bitsy Bahamas and much-bigger Brazil. And this beautiful beige block of eroded salty rock.

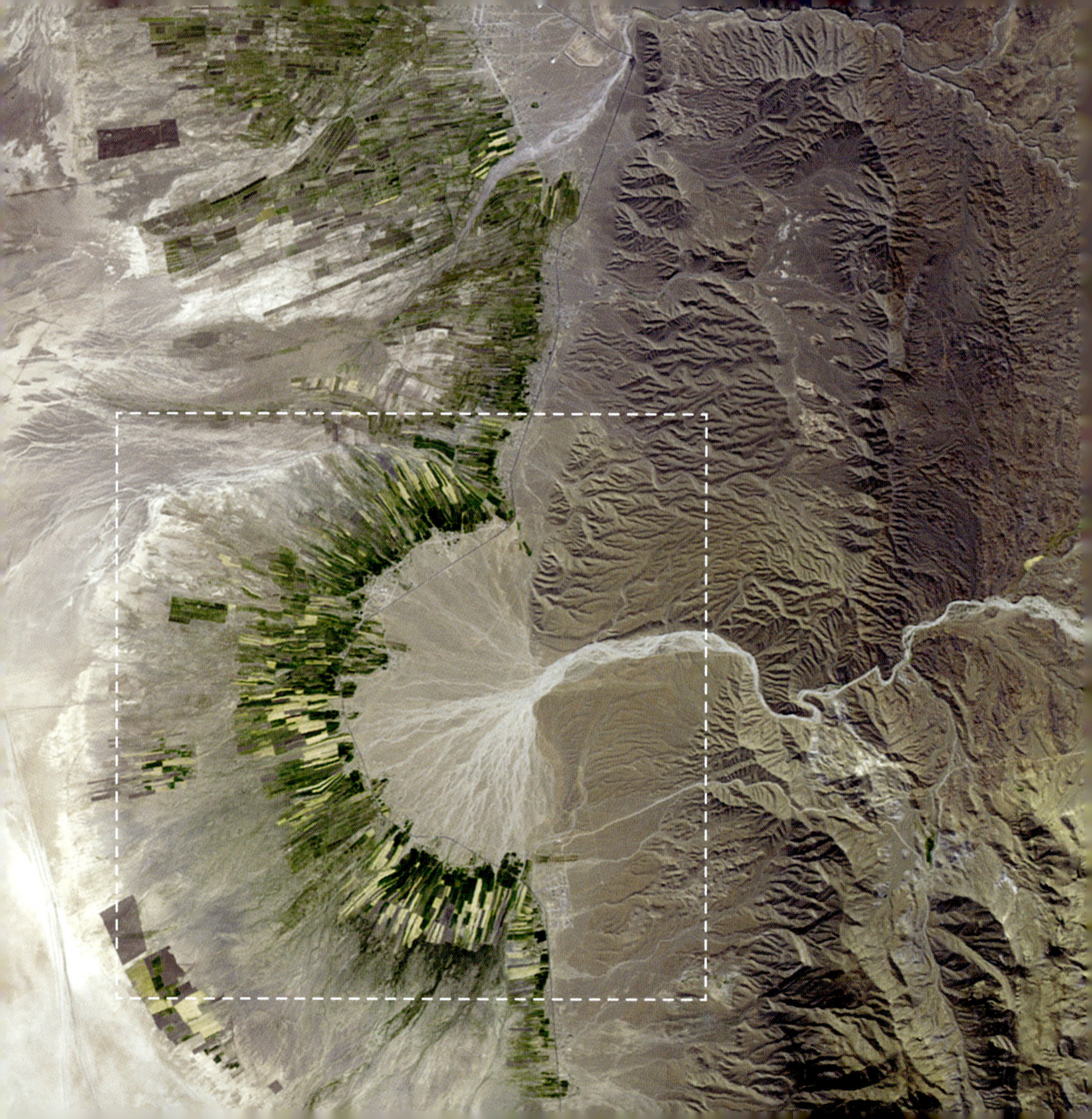

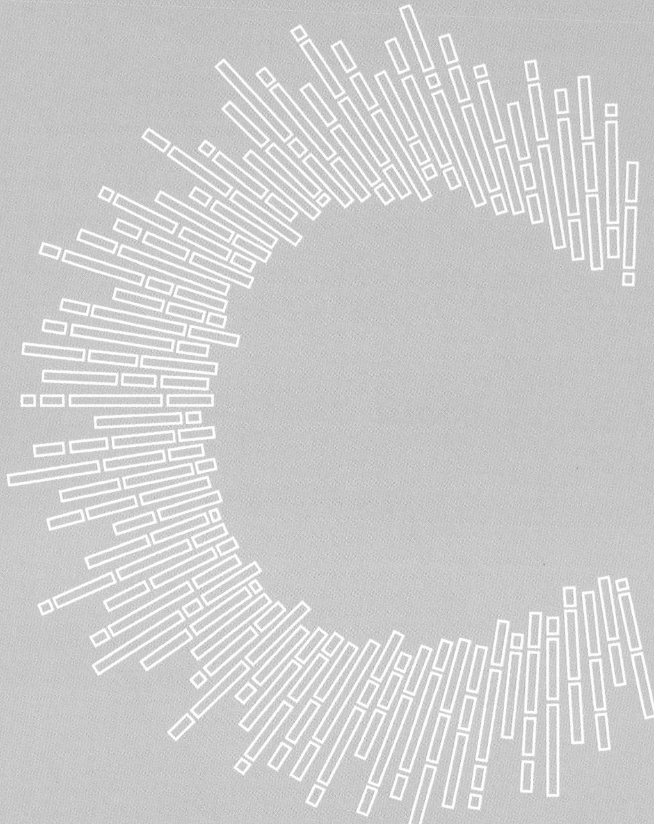

Chin up, **C**! **Craters**, **canyons** and clouds all start with you. So does Cuba and Croatia. And this curved and colourful crescent in Iran caused by crops – maybe corn and crunchy cabbage, or cotton and collards?

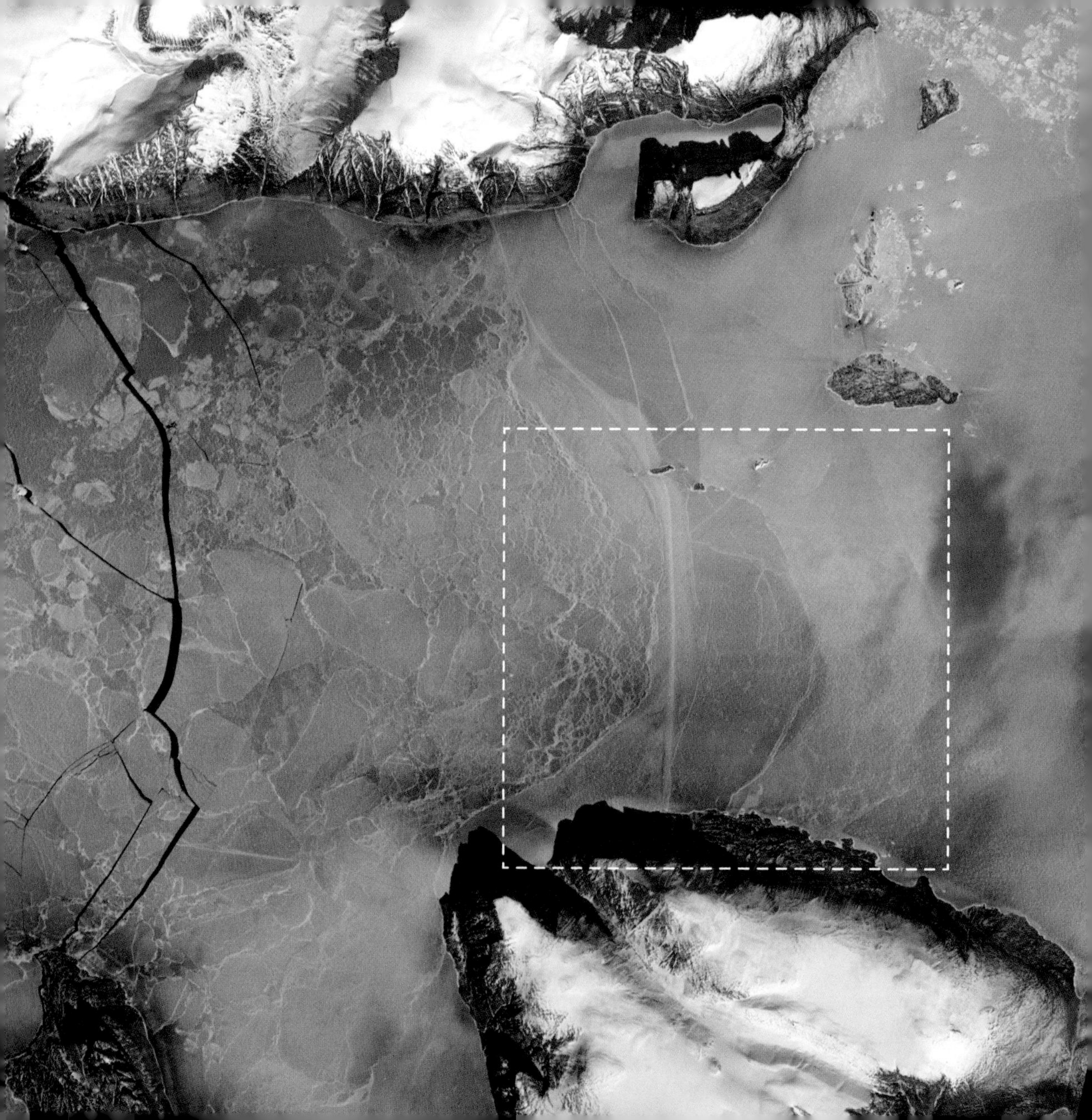

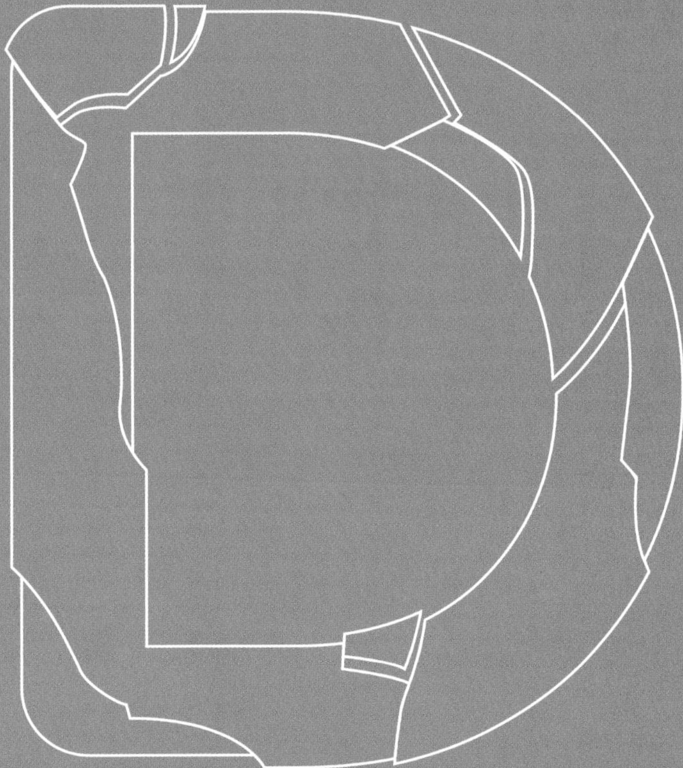

Dear me, it's **D**! Did you know that Denmark and Djibouti begin with D? Deserts, **deltas** and **deforestation** do, too. And these delightful, dazzling divides in the disappearing Arctic sea ice.

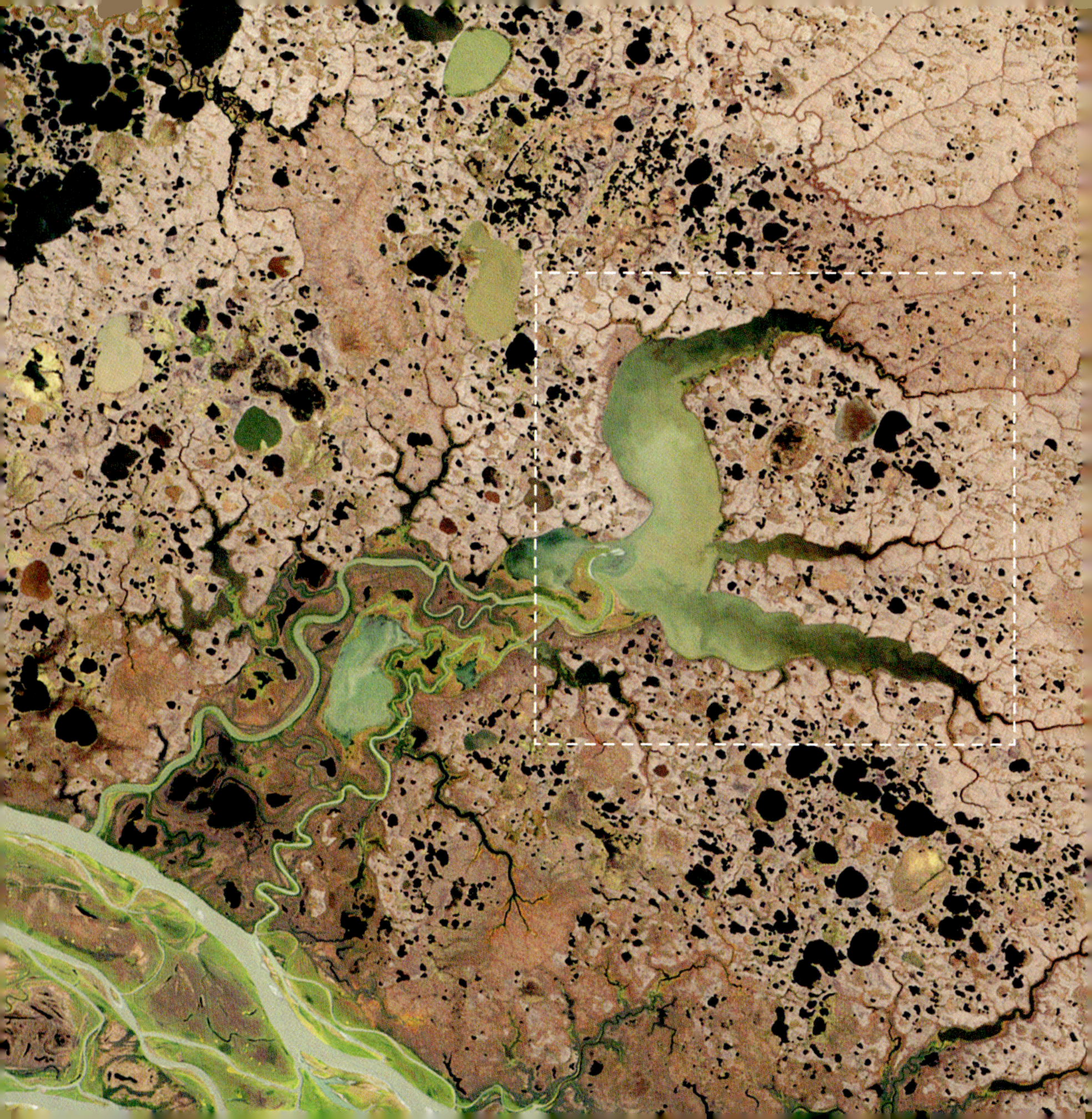

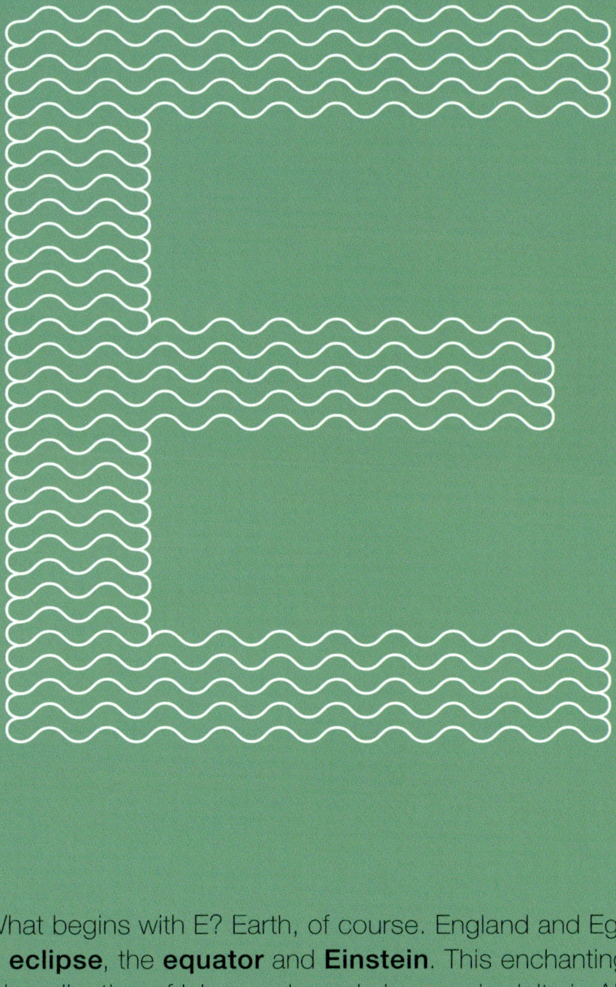

'ello there, **E**. What begins with E? Earth, of course. England and Egypt. **Estuaries** in Estonia. An **eclipse**, the **equator** and **Einstein**. This enchanting image of an eclectic collection of lakes and ponds in an epic delta in Alaska.

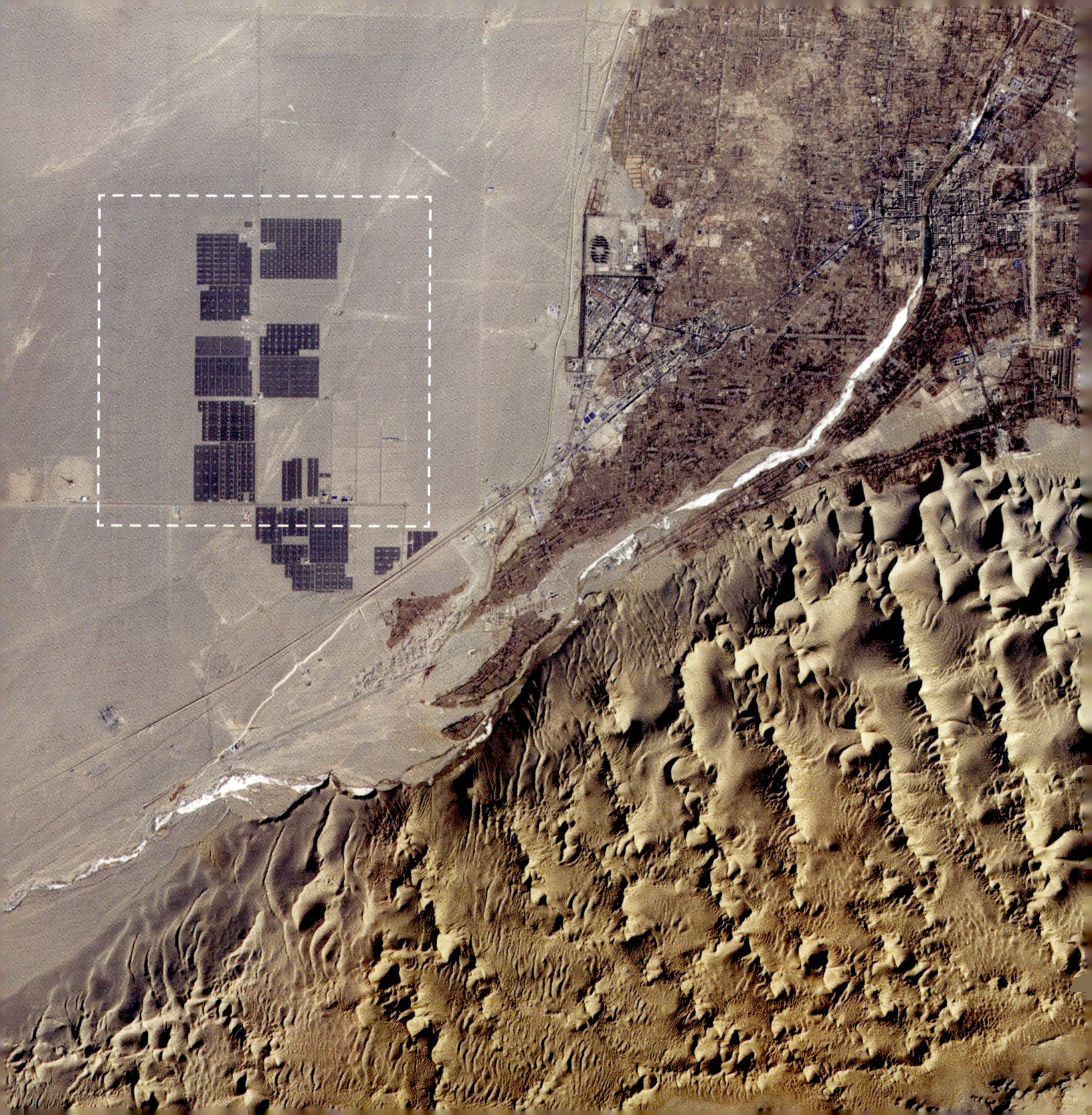

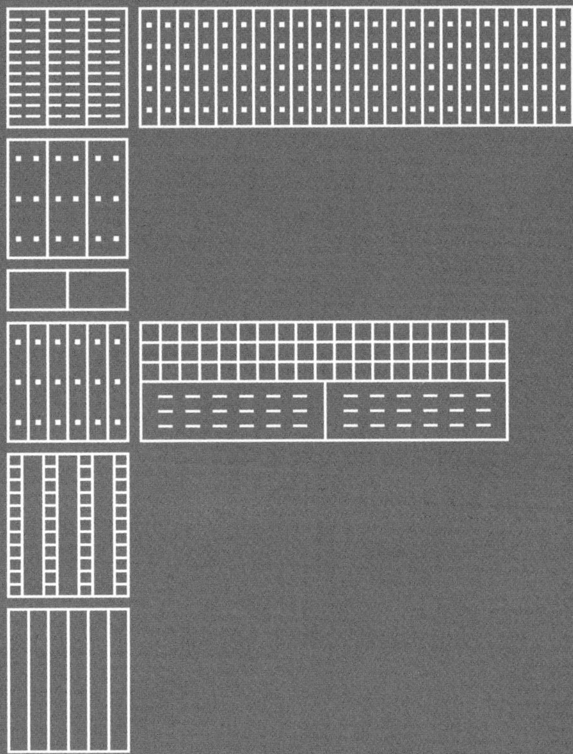

Fancy meeting you, **F**! You are in forests, **fossils** and **frost**.
And also this fast-growing, futuristic solar farm in China's
far-flung Gansu province.

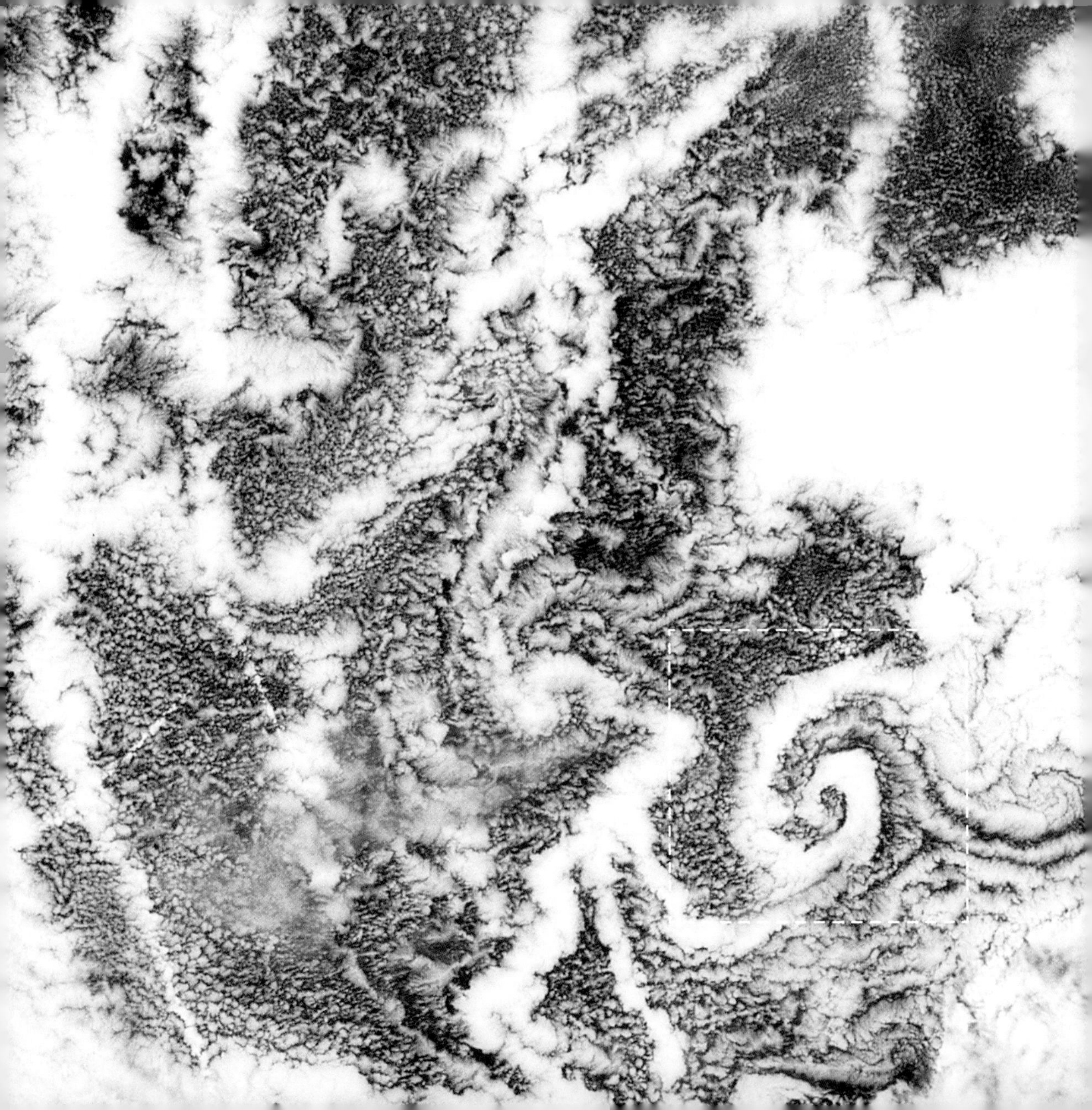

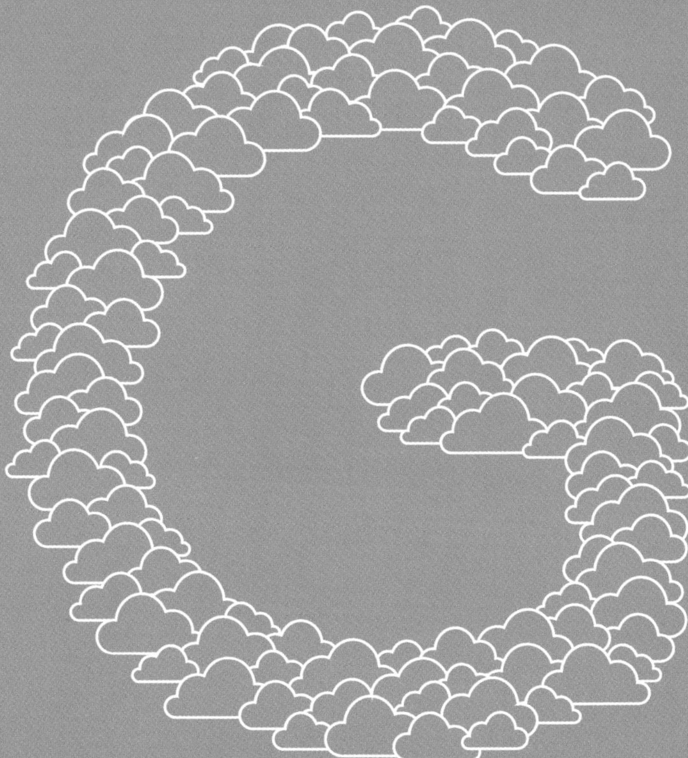

G'day, **G**. What else begins with G? Geology! **Greenhouse gases** and **global warming**. The globe's **glaciers** . . . going, going, gone. These gossamer clouds created by a group of ships gliding across the Pacific like a gaggle of geese.

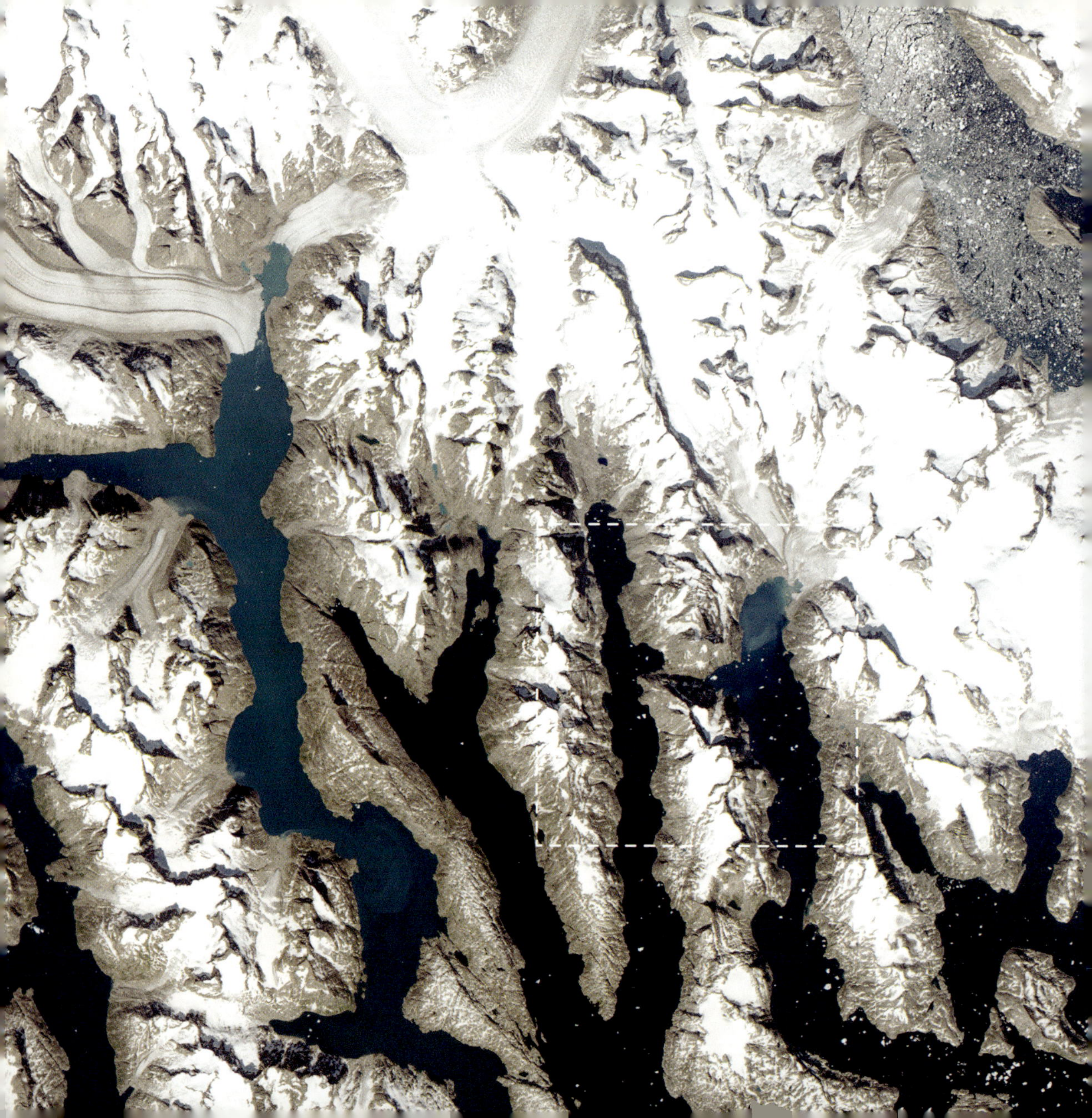

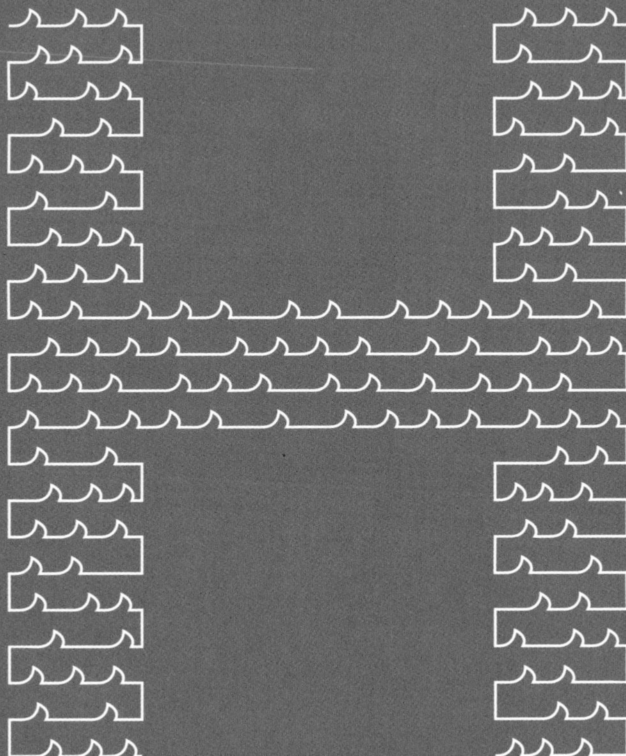

Hola, **H**! Hurricanes and hail begin with H. So do **haze**, heat waves and the **horizon**; Haiti and Hong Kong. Hmmm . . . do you think there are hobbit houses hiding in this heavenly **hydrological** haven tucked between hulking hills?

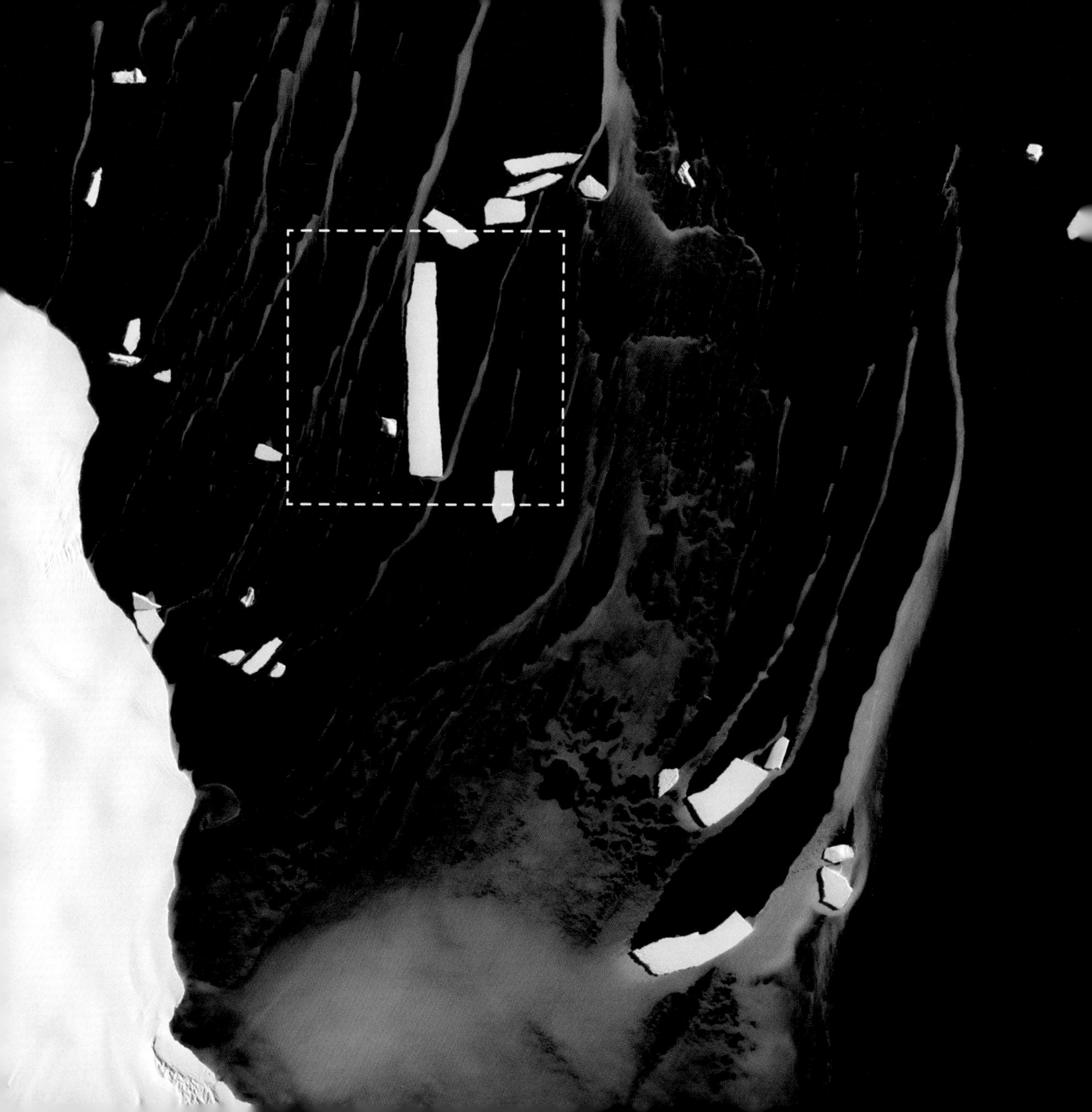

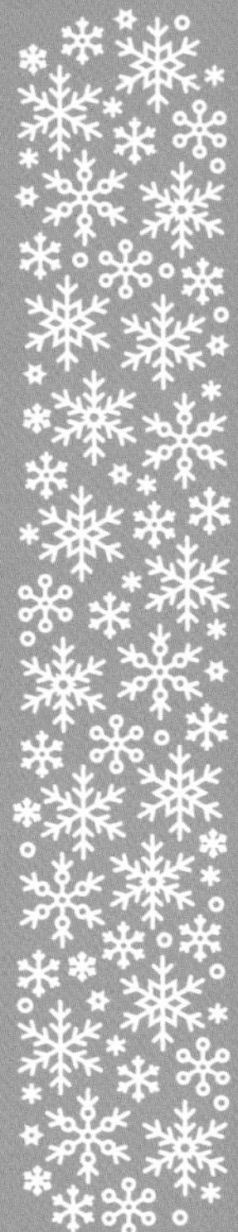

I . . . I . . . I . . . what begins with **I**? India, Israel and Ireland. An **isthmus** in Iceland and intrepid astronauts on the International Space Station. This impeccable iceberg island idling off an **ice shelf** in Antarctica.

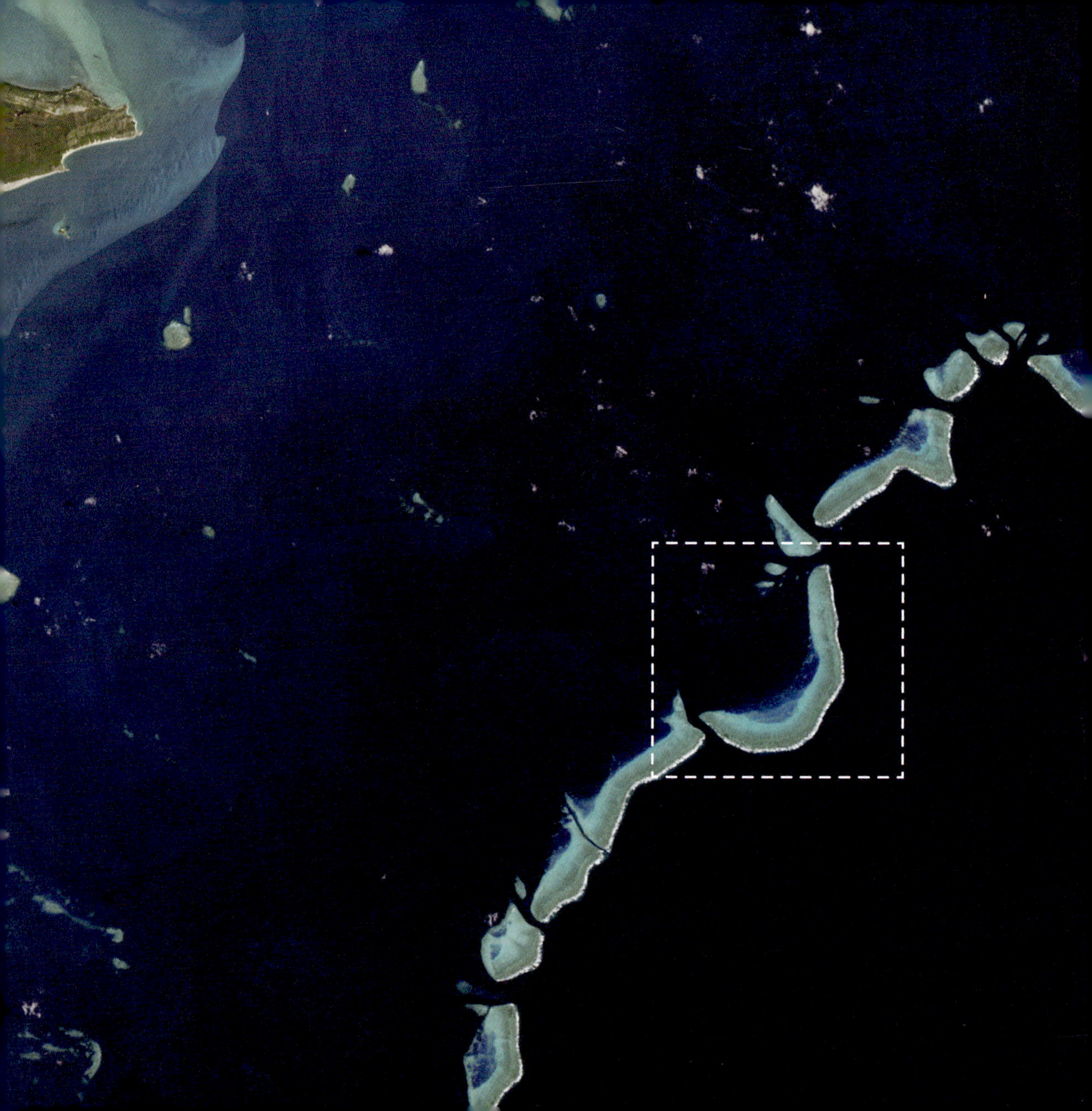

CORAL IN AUSTRALIA'S GREAT BARRIER REEF

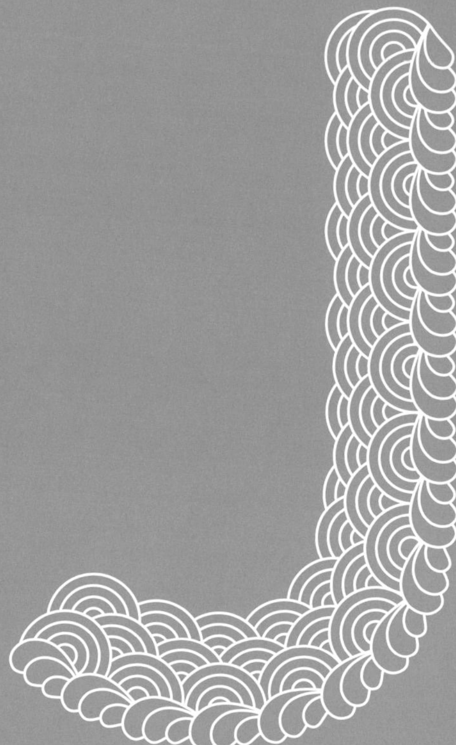

Jeepers, **J**! Japan and Jamaica start with you. So does the **jet stream** and **Johnson Space Center**. Don't you want to jump for joy upon seeing this jade-coloured coral reef juxtaposed against the sea?

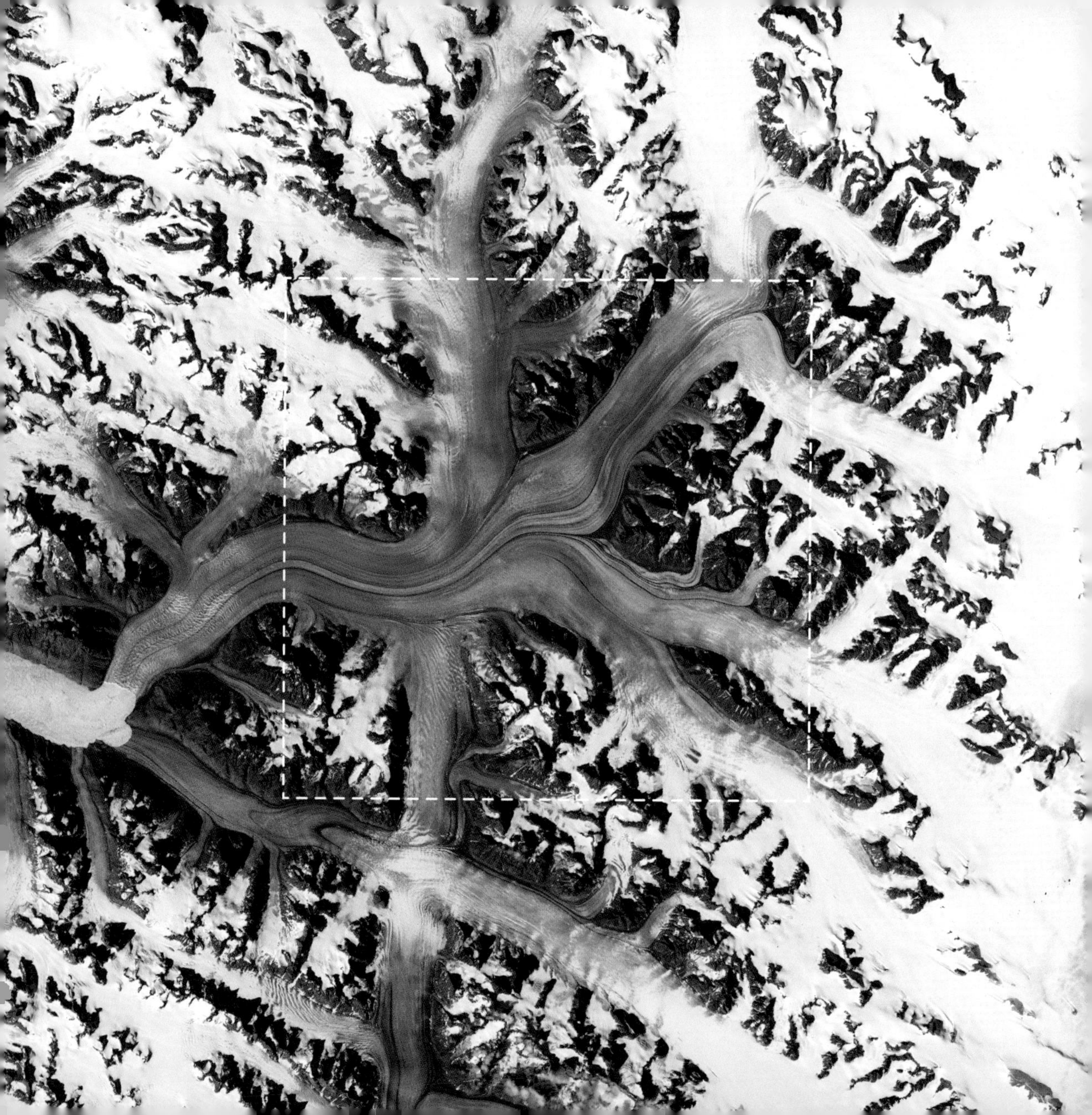

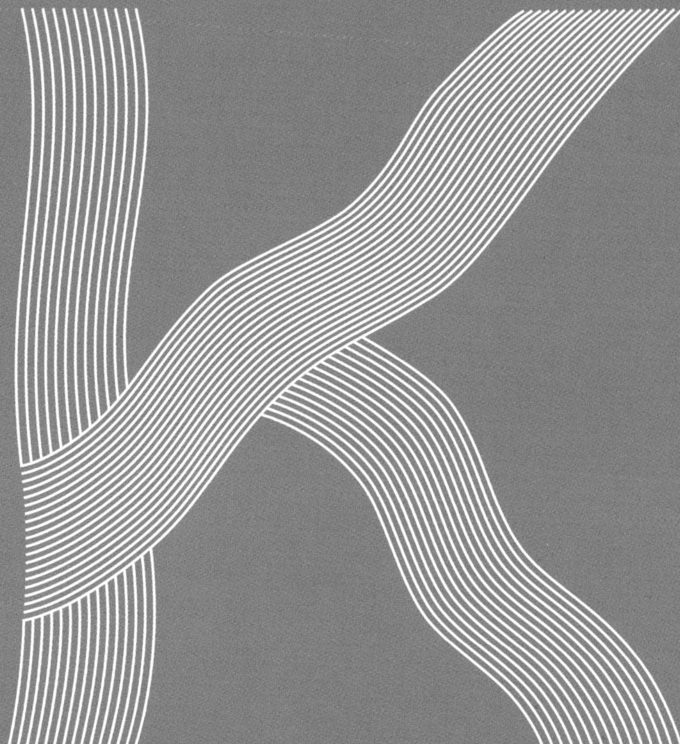

Konichiwa, **K**! **Kettle ponds** and **kelp** are K words. Kenya and Kazakhstan. **Katabatic winds** stronger than a kangaroo's kick to your kidney careening down icy glaciers towards the sea.

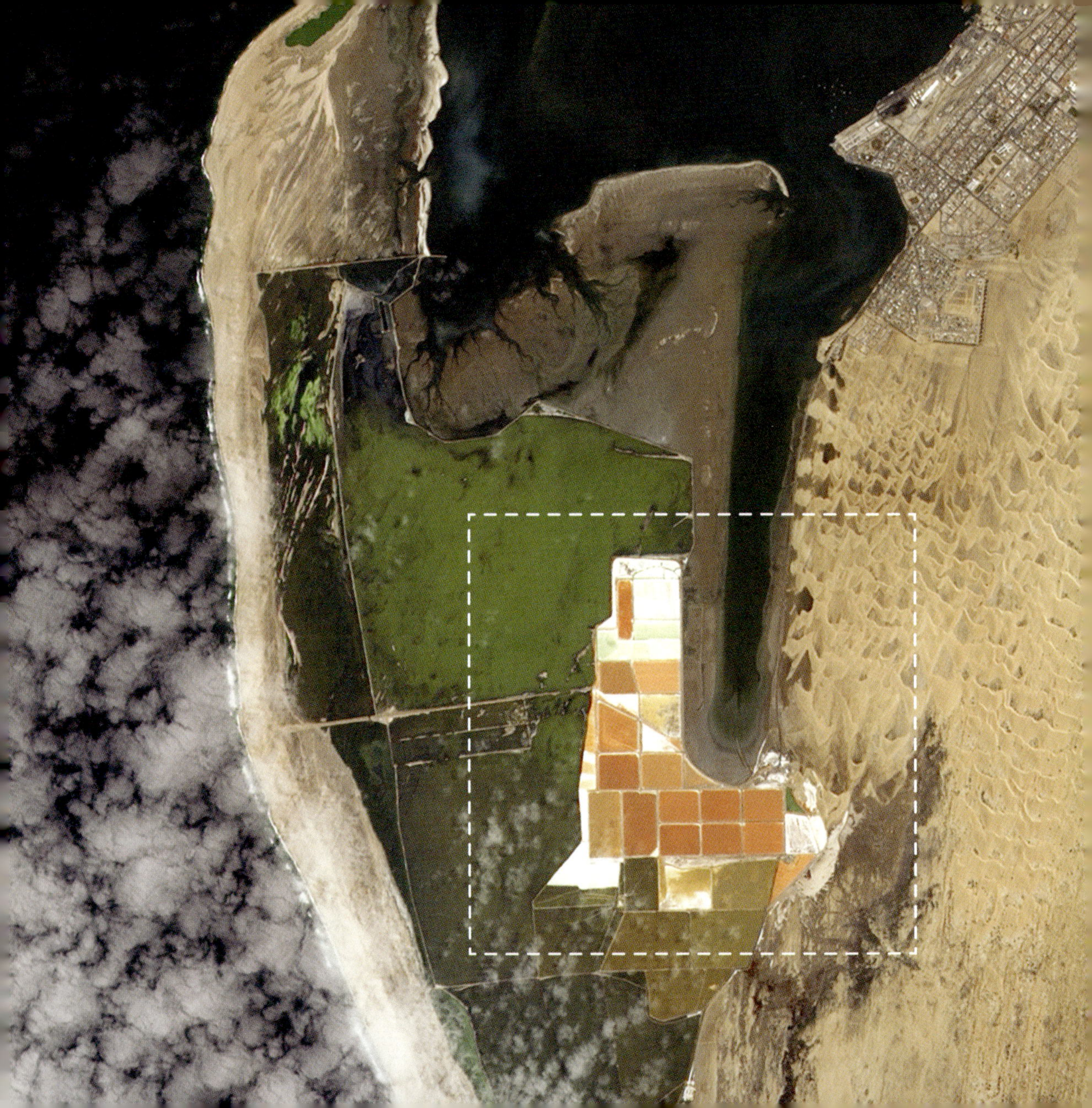

Lo and behold, it's **L**. What begins with L? **Lava lakes** and lightning. Laos, Lithuania and London. Please just look, don't lick these light-orange lakes loaded with salt!

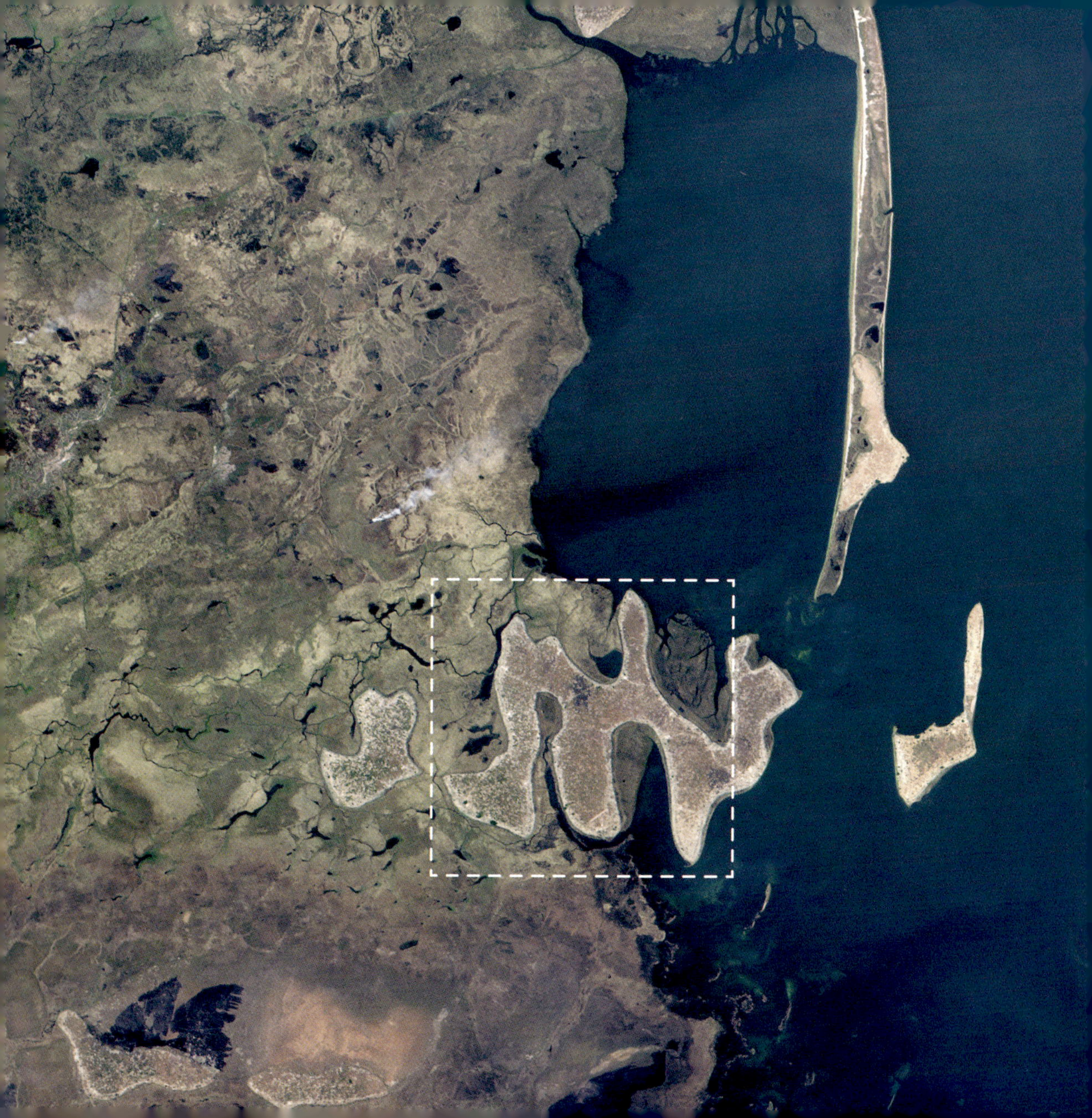

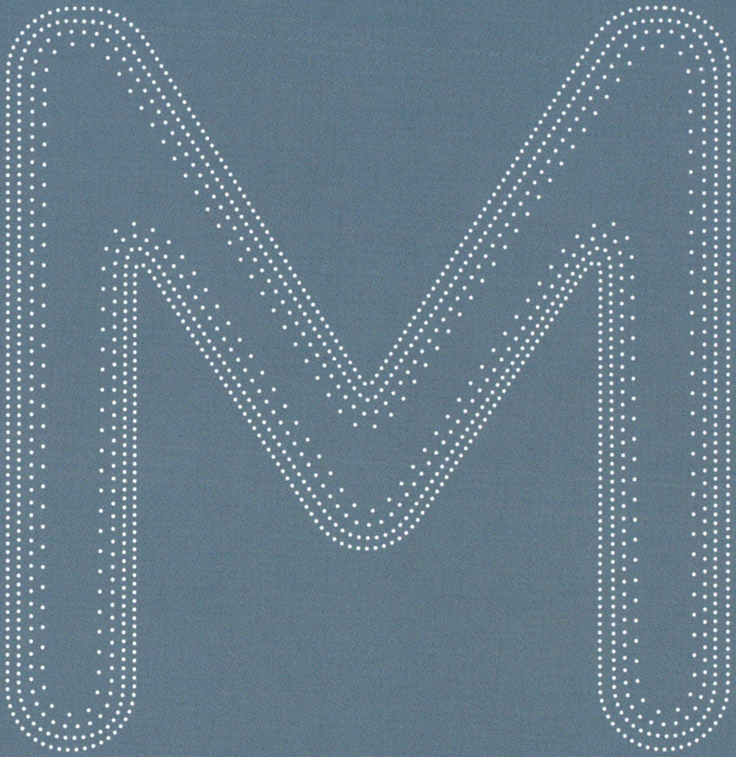

ISLAND IN ZAMBIA'S LAKE BANGWEULU

Mwah, mwah, mwah, it's **M**! The muddy **meandering** Mississippi has some M's. **Magma**, **meteors** and **mammatus clouds** have a few, too. And, of course, there's this magnificent and marshy island made of mud and sand.

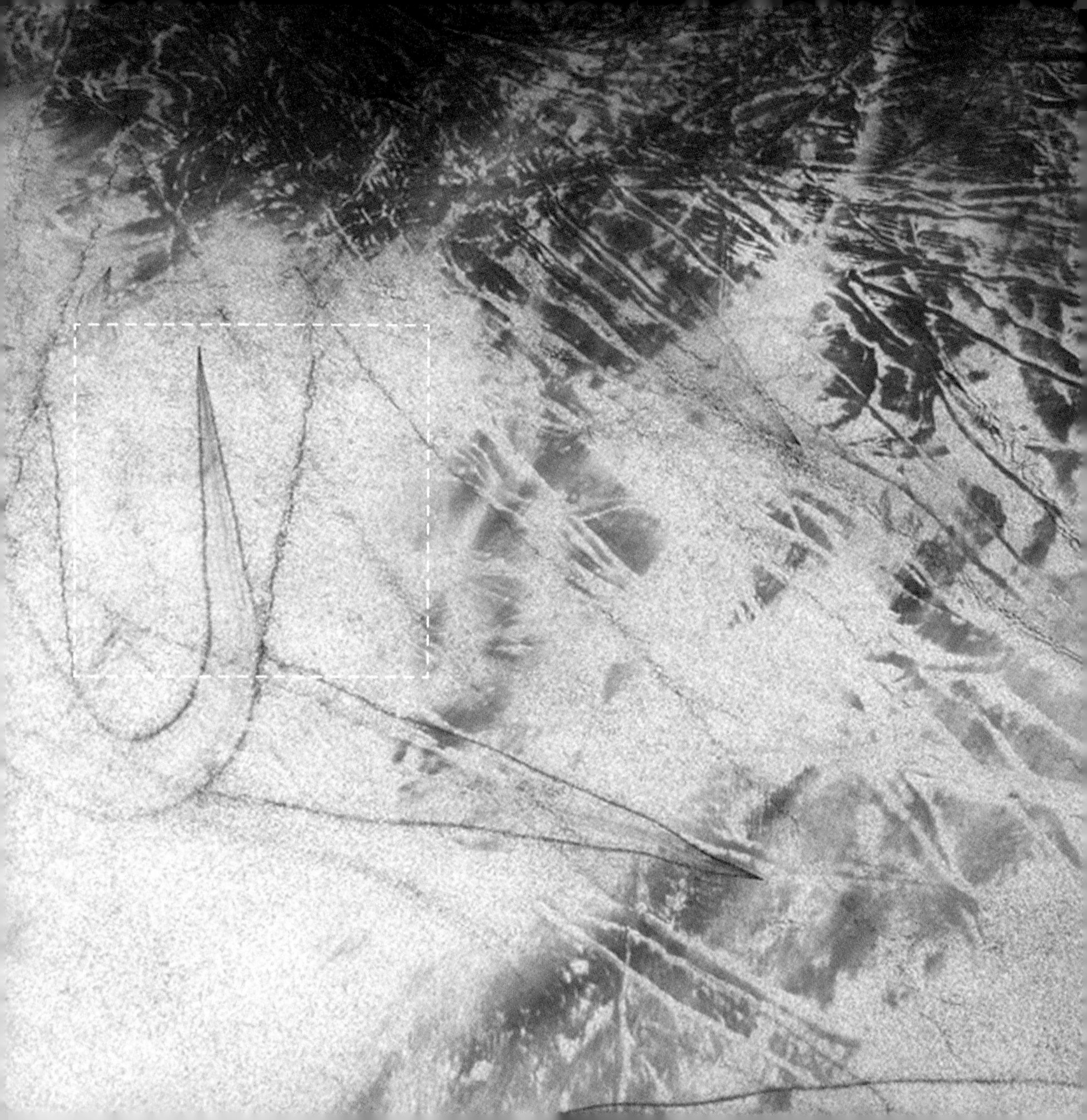

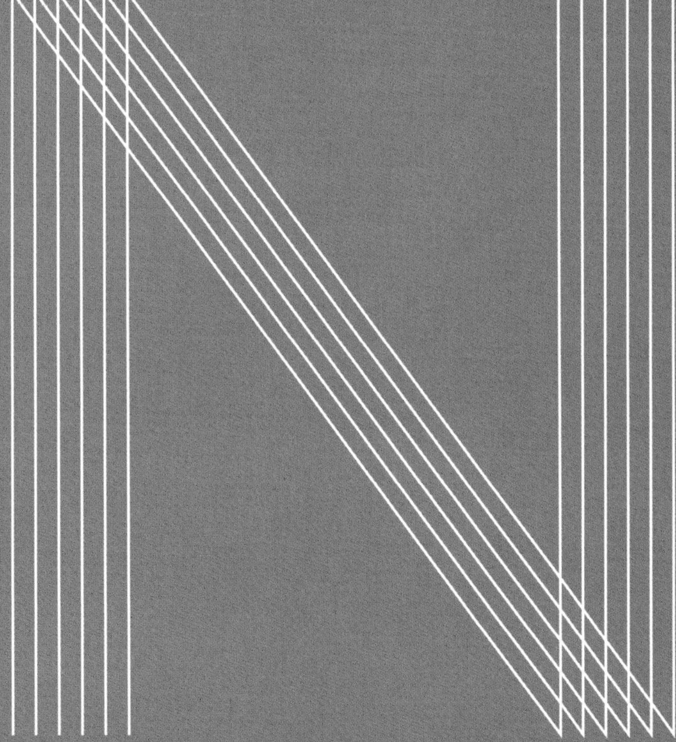

Namaste, **N**. What begins with N? The Nile River, the North Pole and Nepal. NASA and **Newton**. The noses of numerous boats nimbly navigating this nifty North American lake.

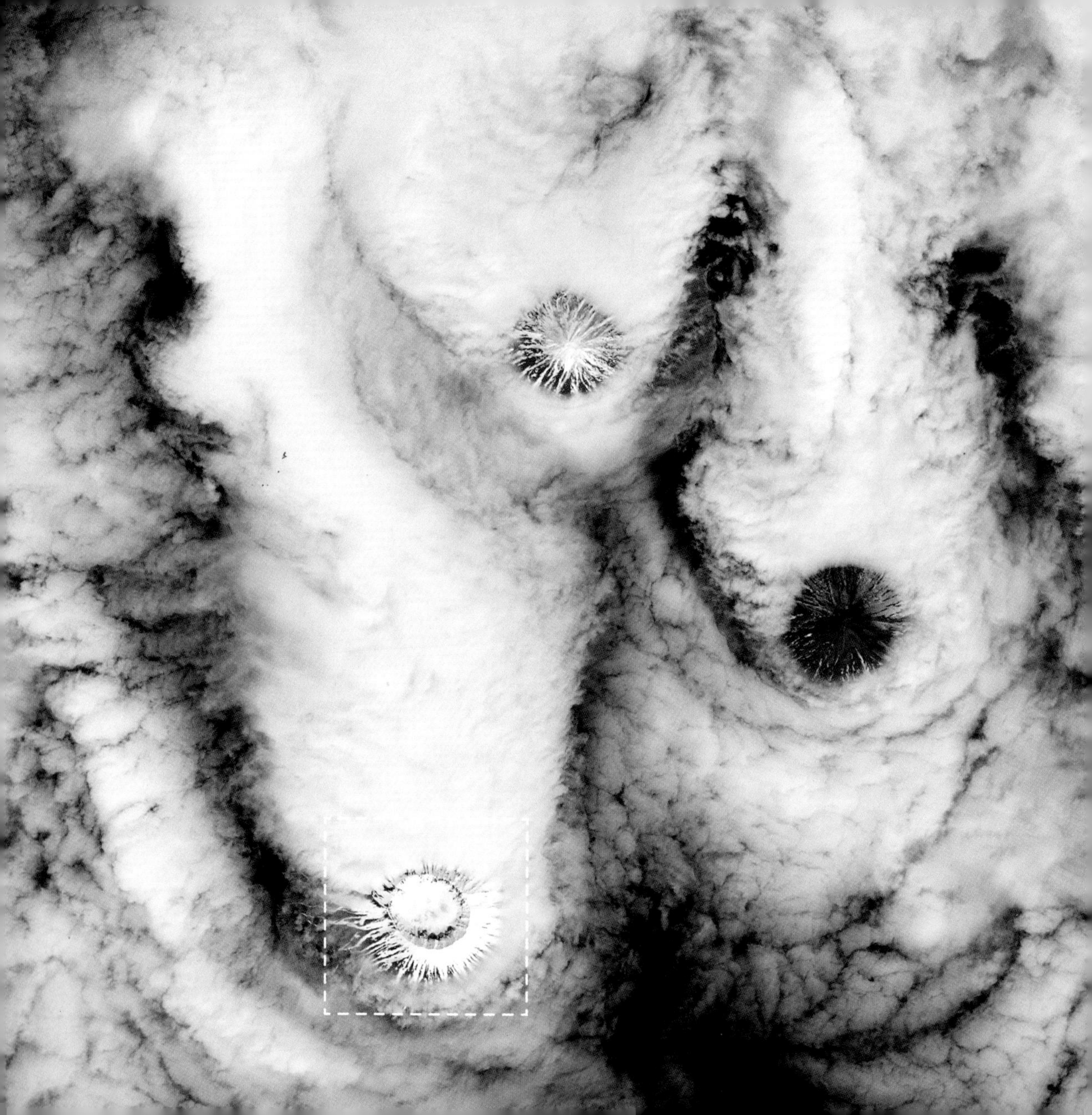

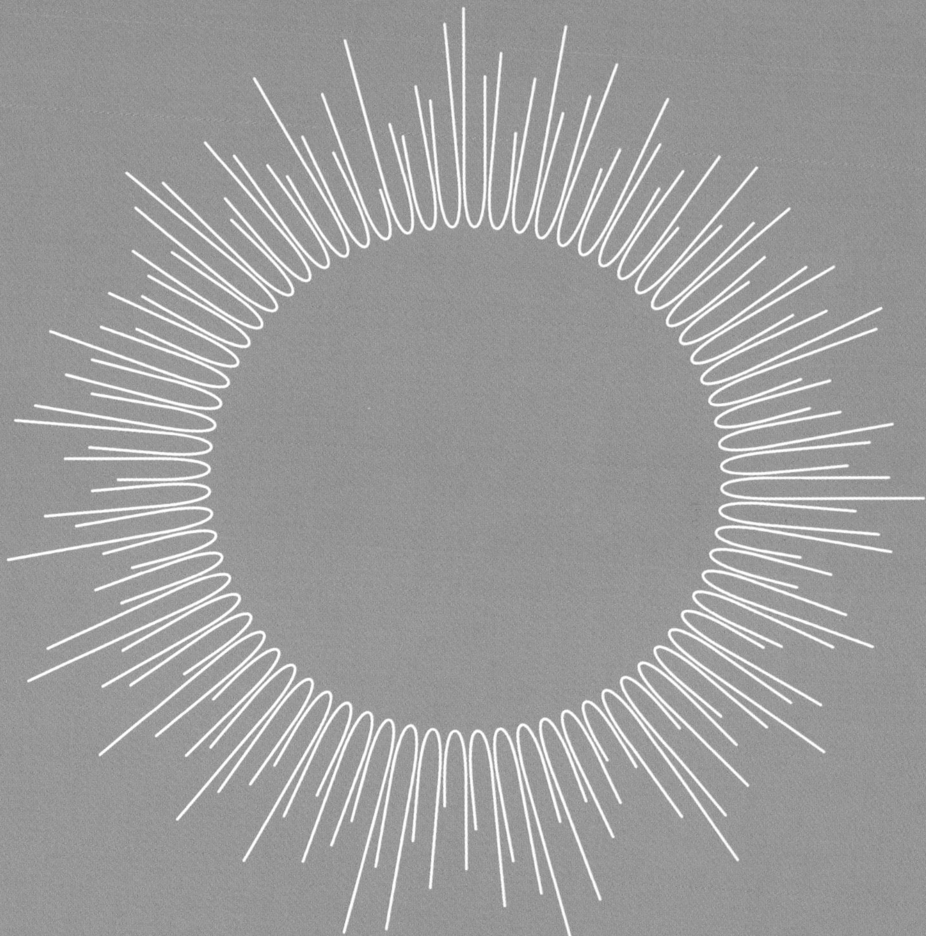

Oh my, it's **O**. **Ooids** in the ocean have plenty of O's. Oman, Oxford and Okinawa. These outstanding oversized volcano peaks ousting clouds out of the way on an overcast day.

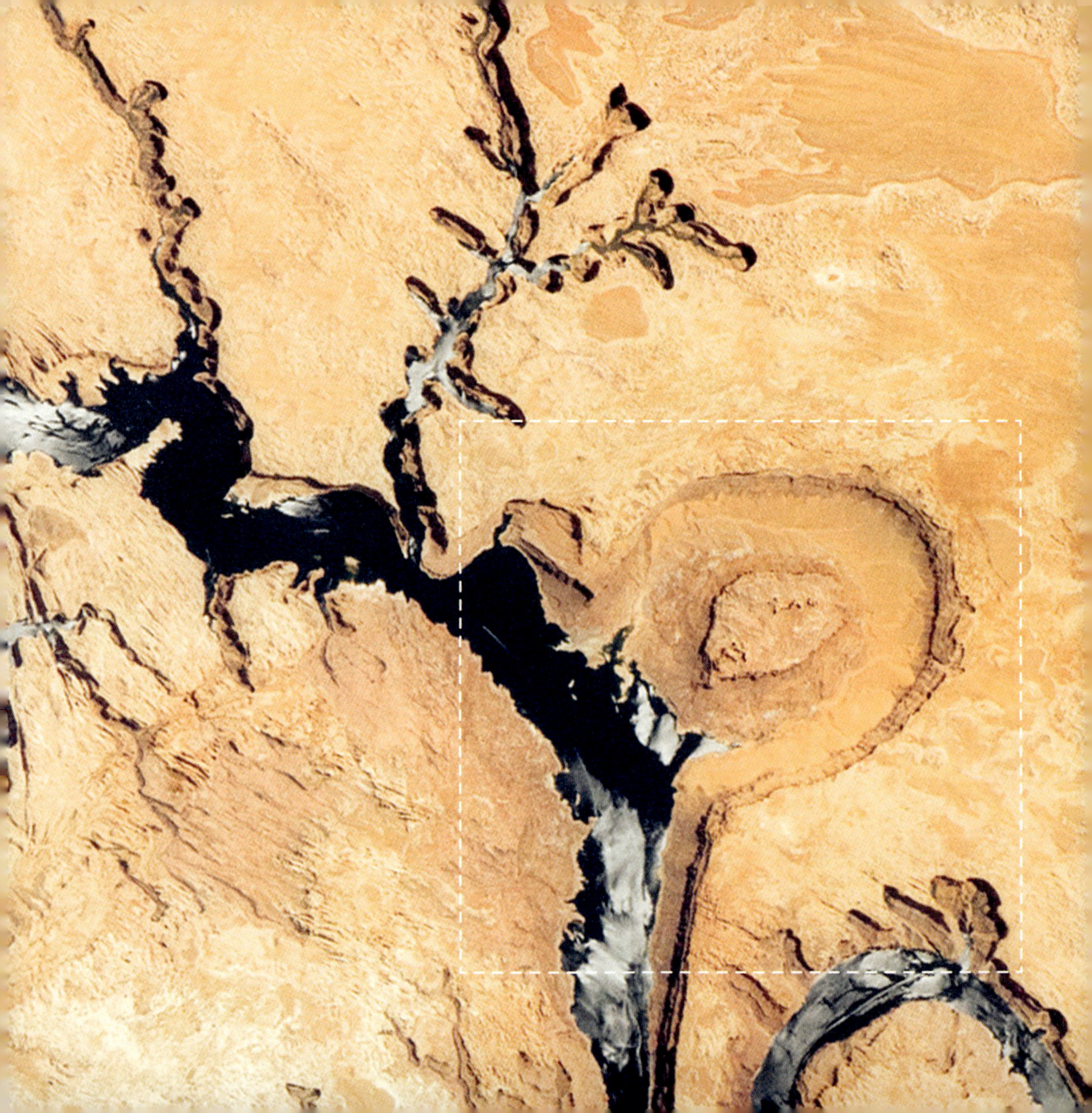

Psssst, it's **P**! **Pancake ice**, **plateaus** and planets all begin with P. So do Panama and Paris. And this puzzling portion of Lake Powell where water and rock peacefully part.

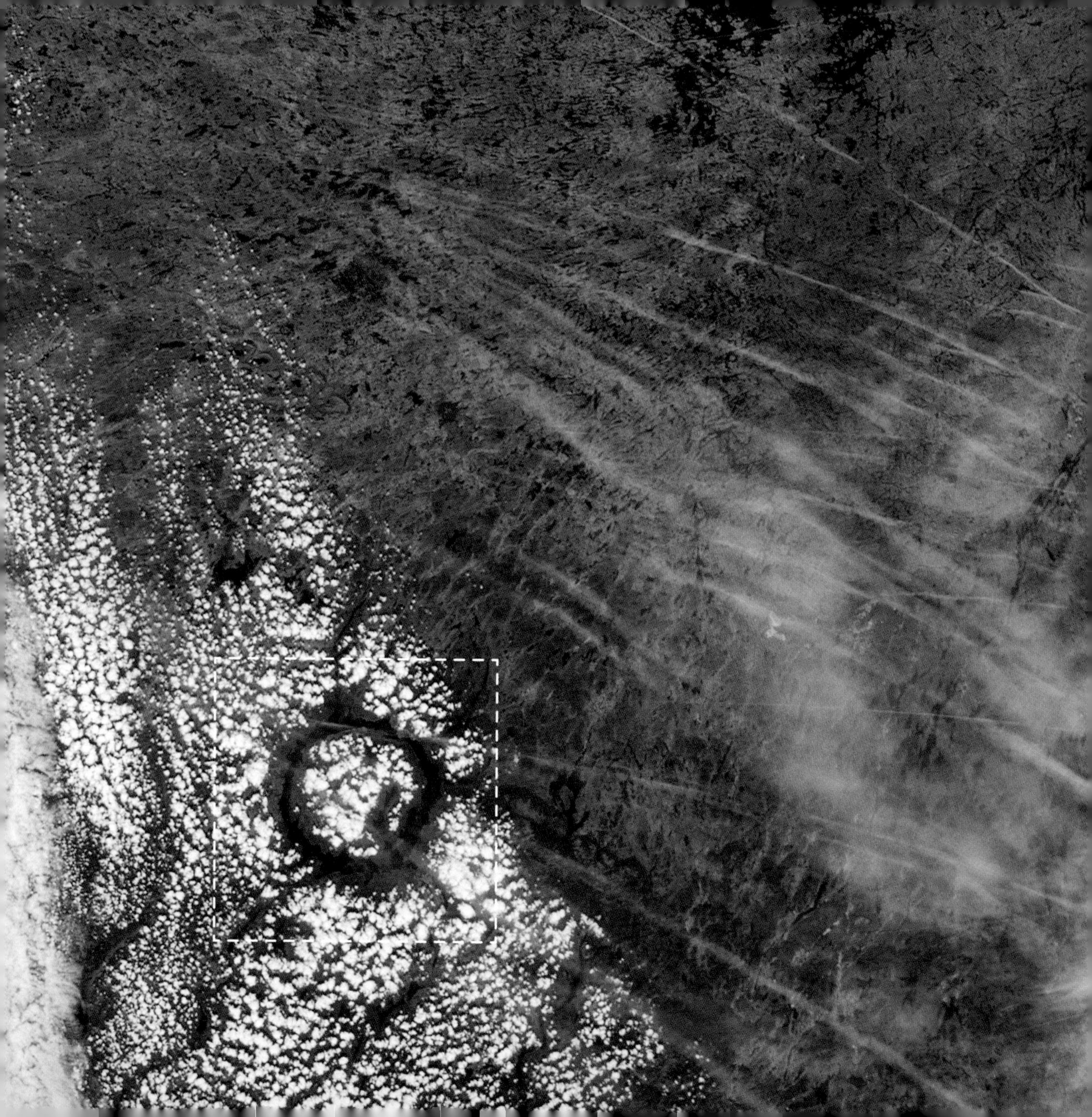

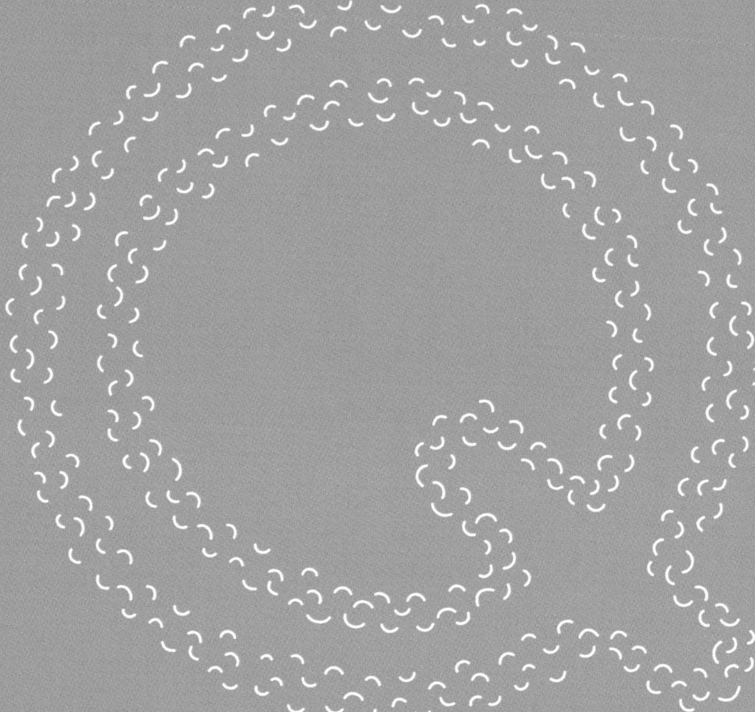

Quick, what begins with **Q**? Qatar, Quebec and Quito in Ecuador. **Quantum theory** and the **Quaternary Period**. The quirky quartz in this lake with quite a queer shape!

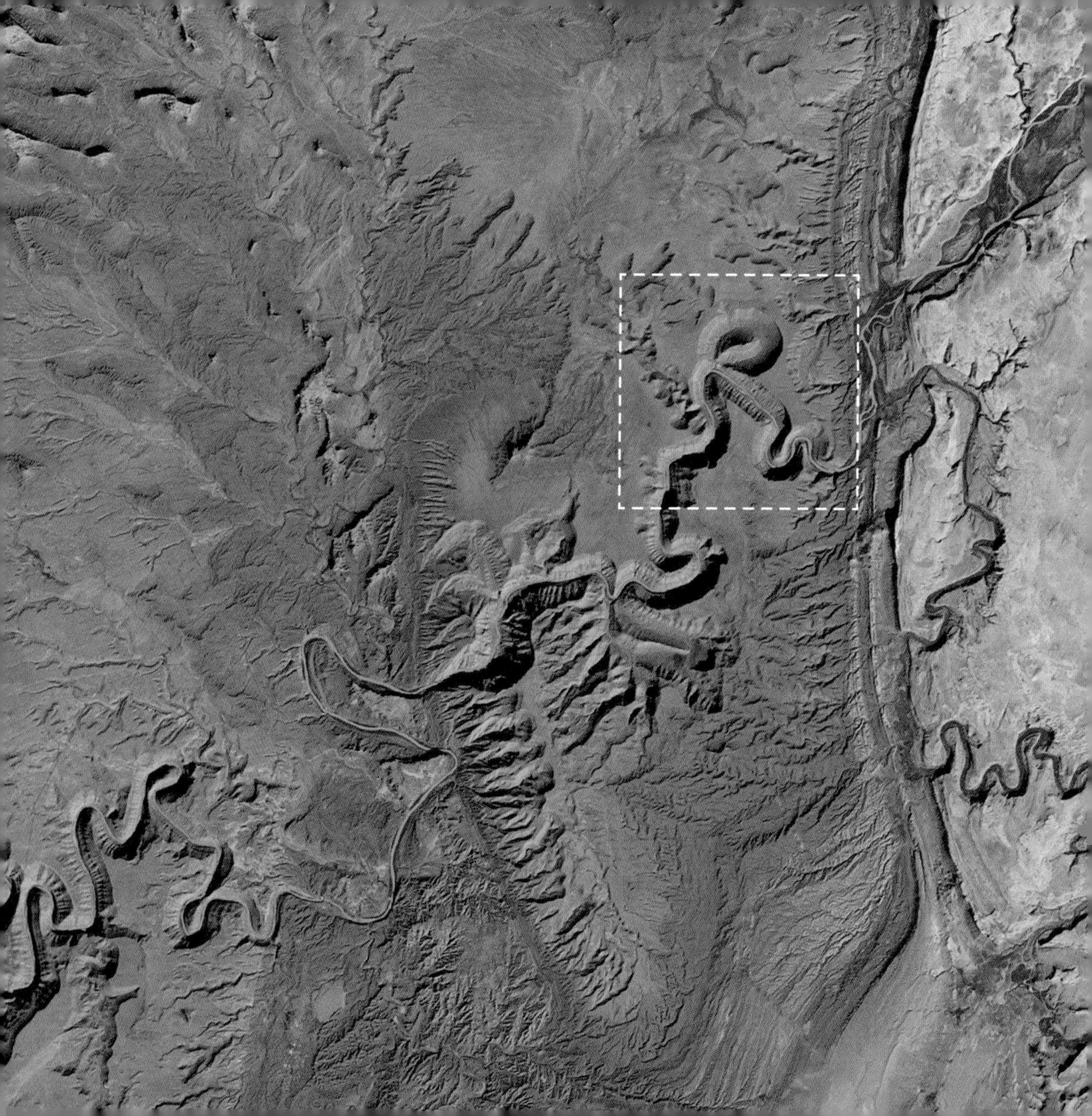

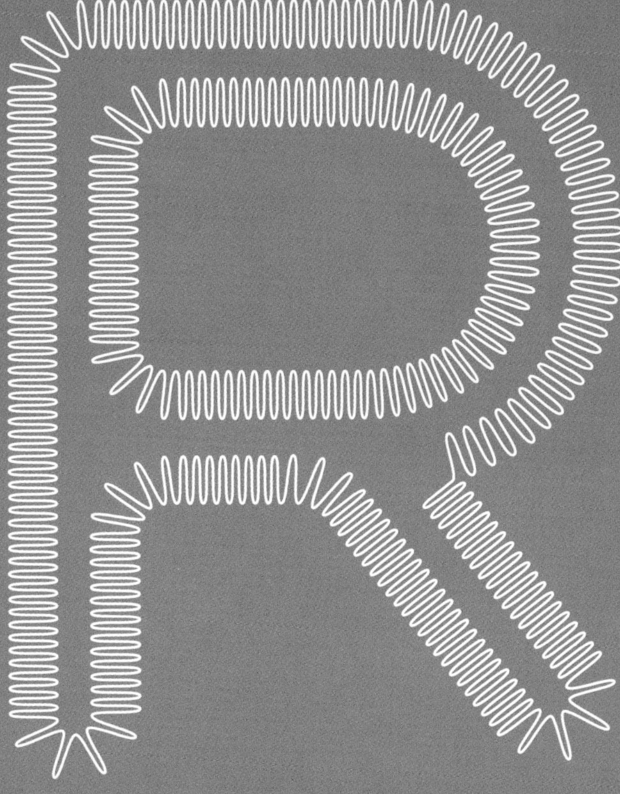

Right on, **R**. Rocket, **radar** and river begin with R. **Rainforests** in Rwanda and **reefs** in the Red Sea. This resplendent river canyon wriggling through rural Utah like a writhing rattlesnake.

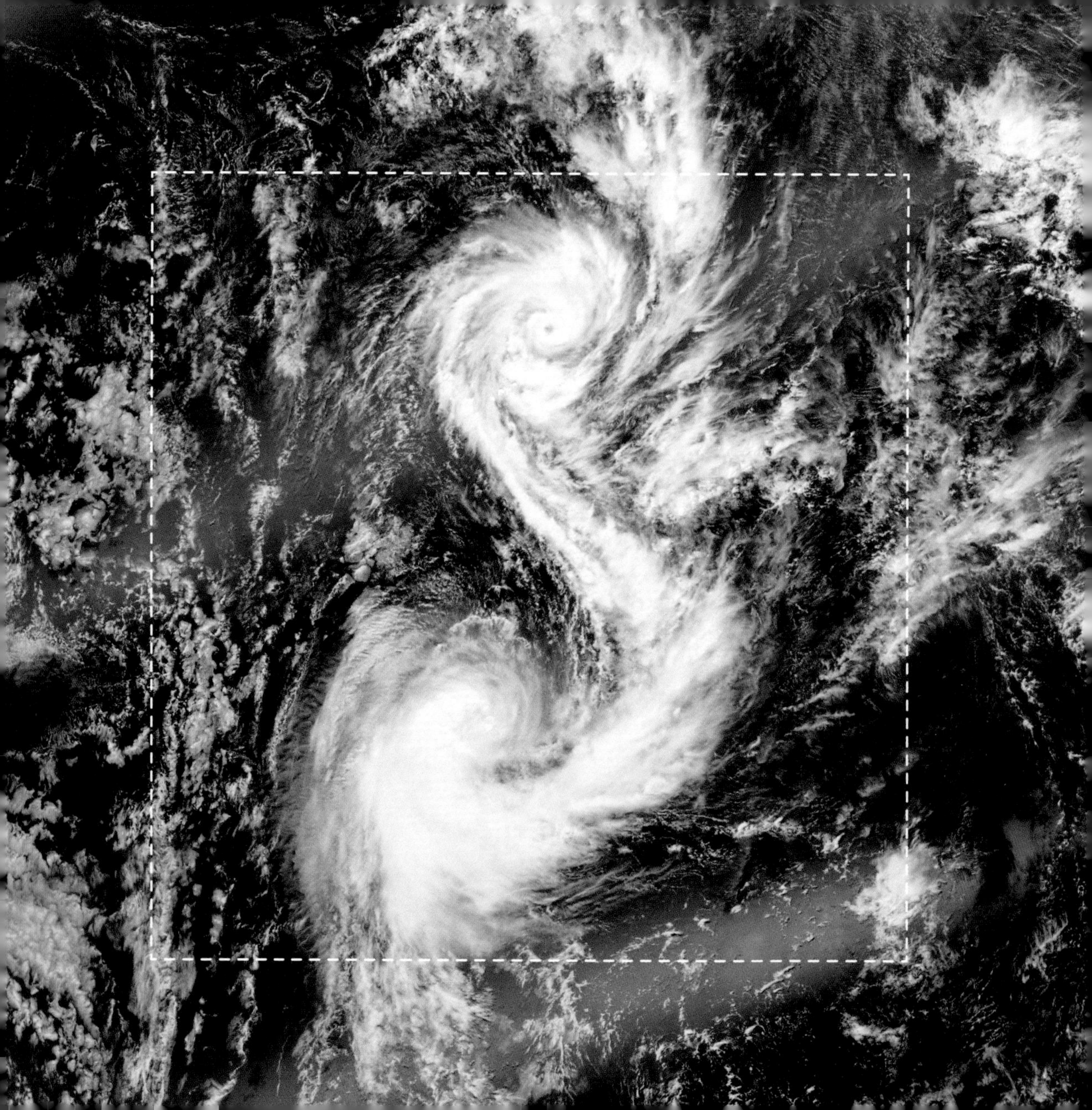

Shazaam, it's **S**! What begins with S? Syria and Switzerland. Sand dunes in Saudi Arabia, **savannas** in Sudan, and **satellites** in space! These spectacular storm clouds swirling over seriously savage seas.

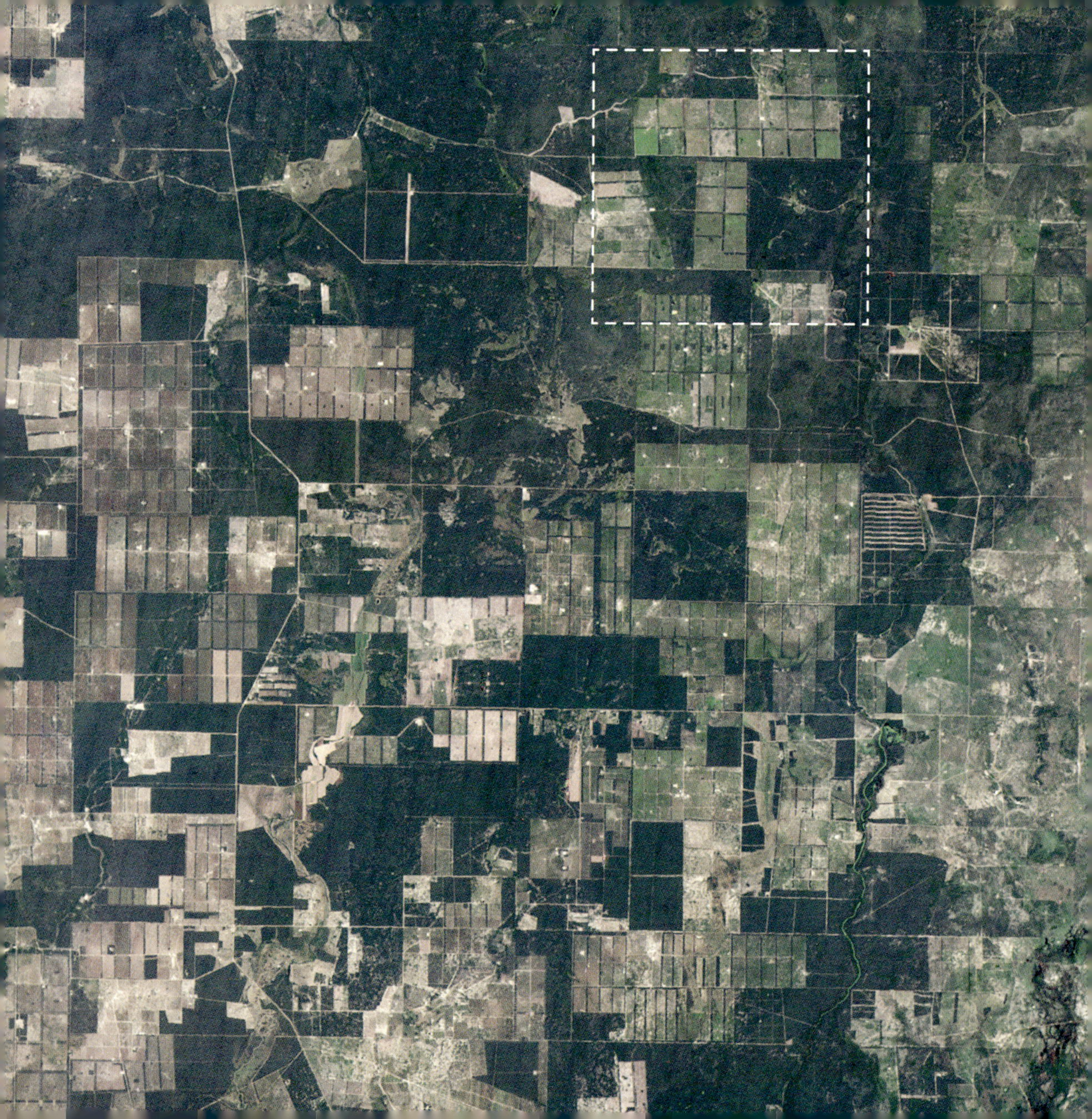

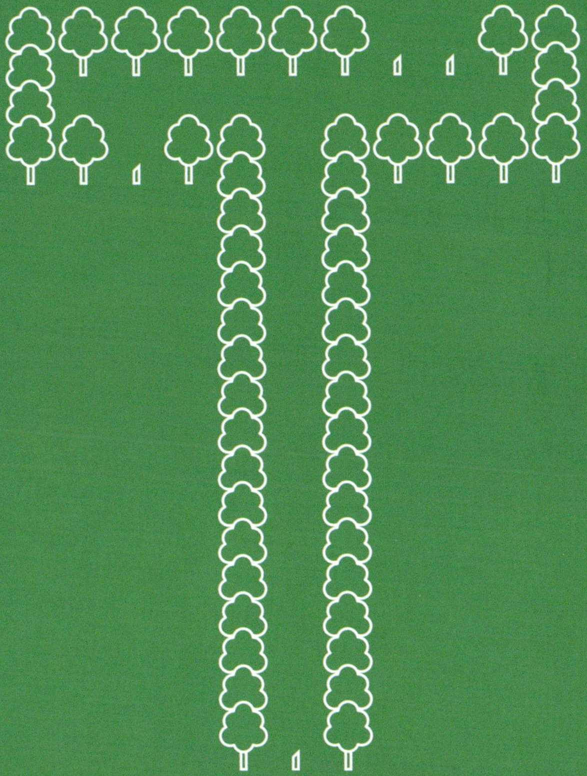

Tally-ho, **T**. You start off tornadoes, **typhoons** and thunderstorms. Tanzania, Thailand and Turkey, too. The thwack, thunk and thud of tumbling tree trunks transformed this green forested terrain to a tawny-tan colour.

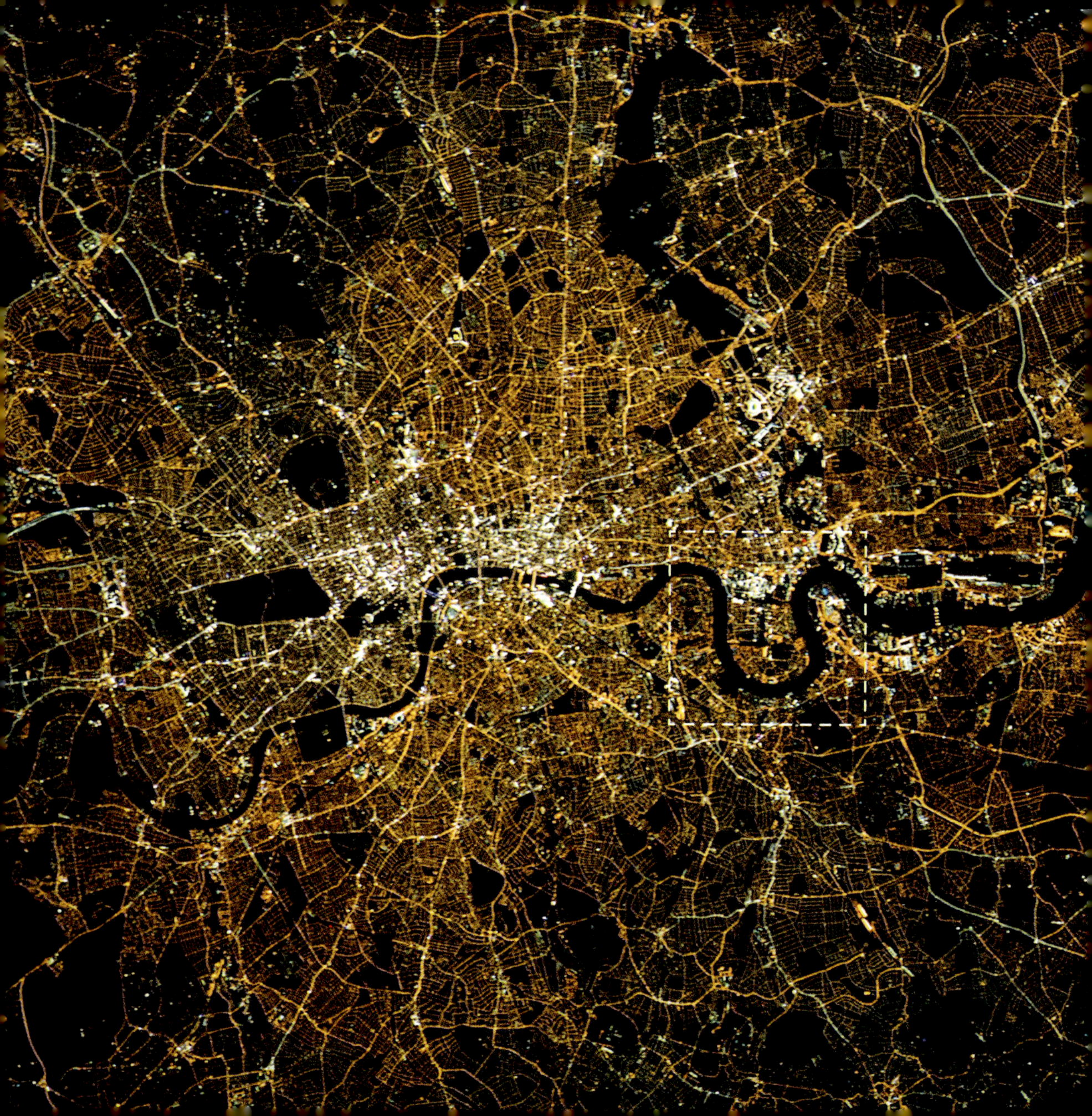

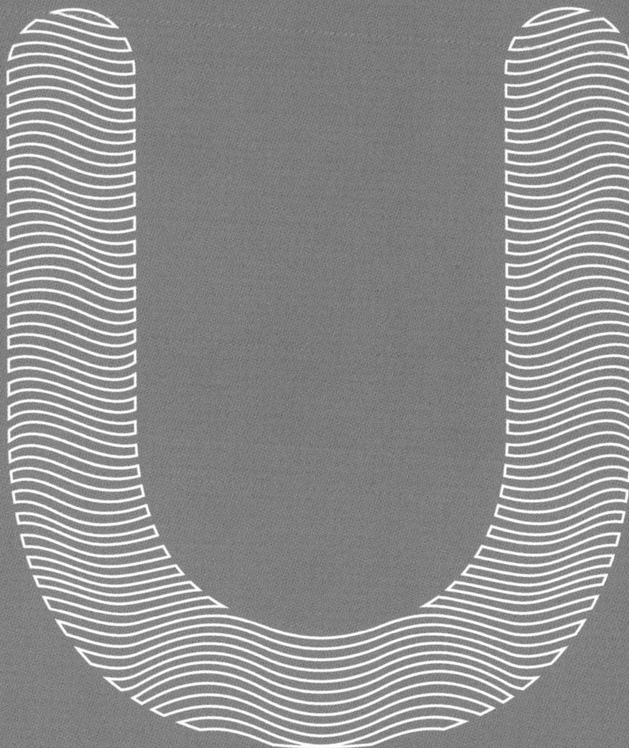

Ummmm, what begins with **U**? The United Kingdom, Uganda and Uzbekistan. **Undertows** and ocean **upwelling**. The unparalleled urban lights of London at night – unquestionably umami for the eyes!

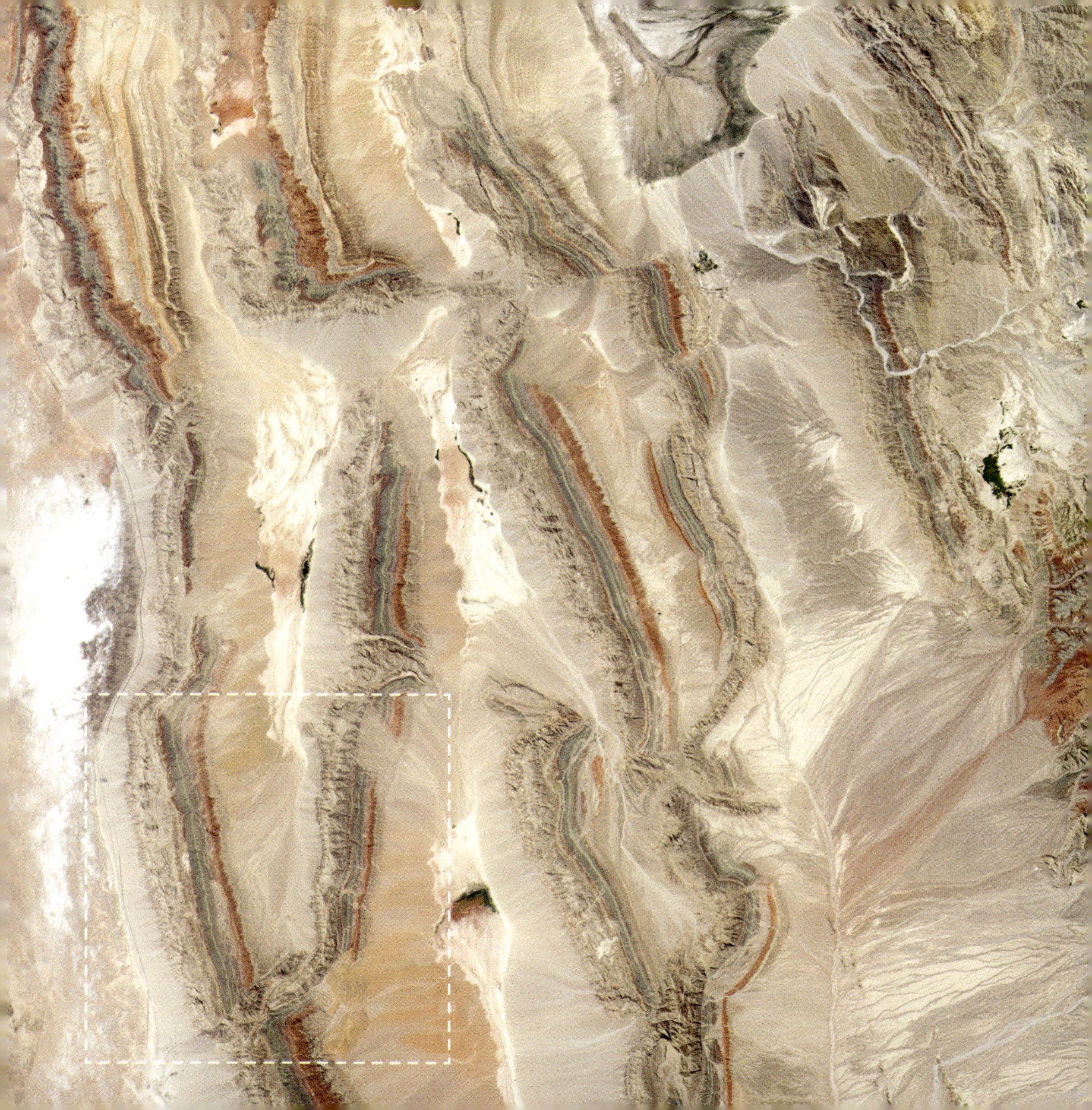

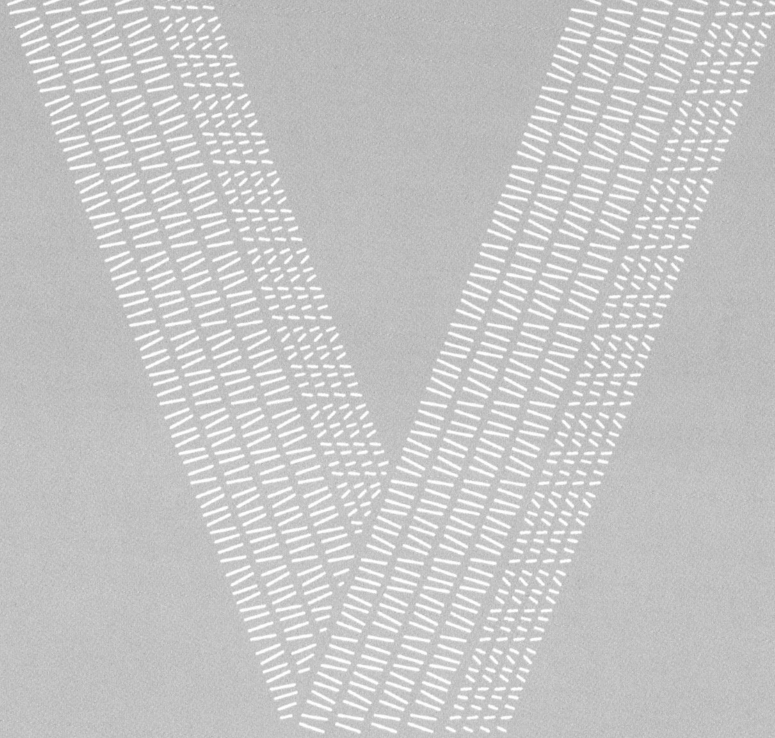

Voilà, **V**! **Volcanoes**, valleys and **vog** begin with V.
Vietnam and Venezuela. These vast, vivid, vermilion valley walls
veering into the desert void in China.

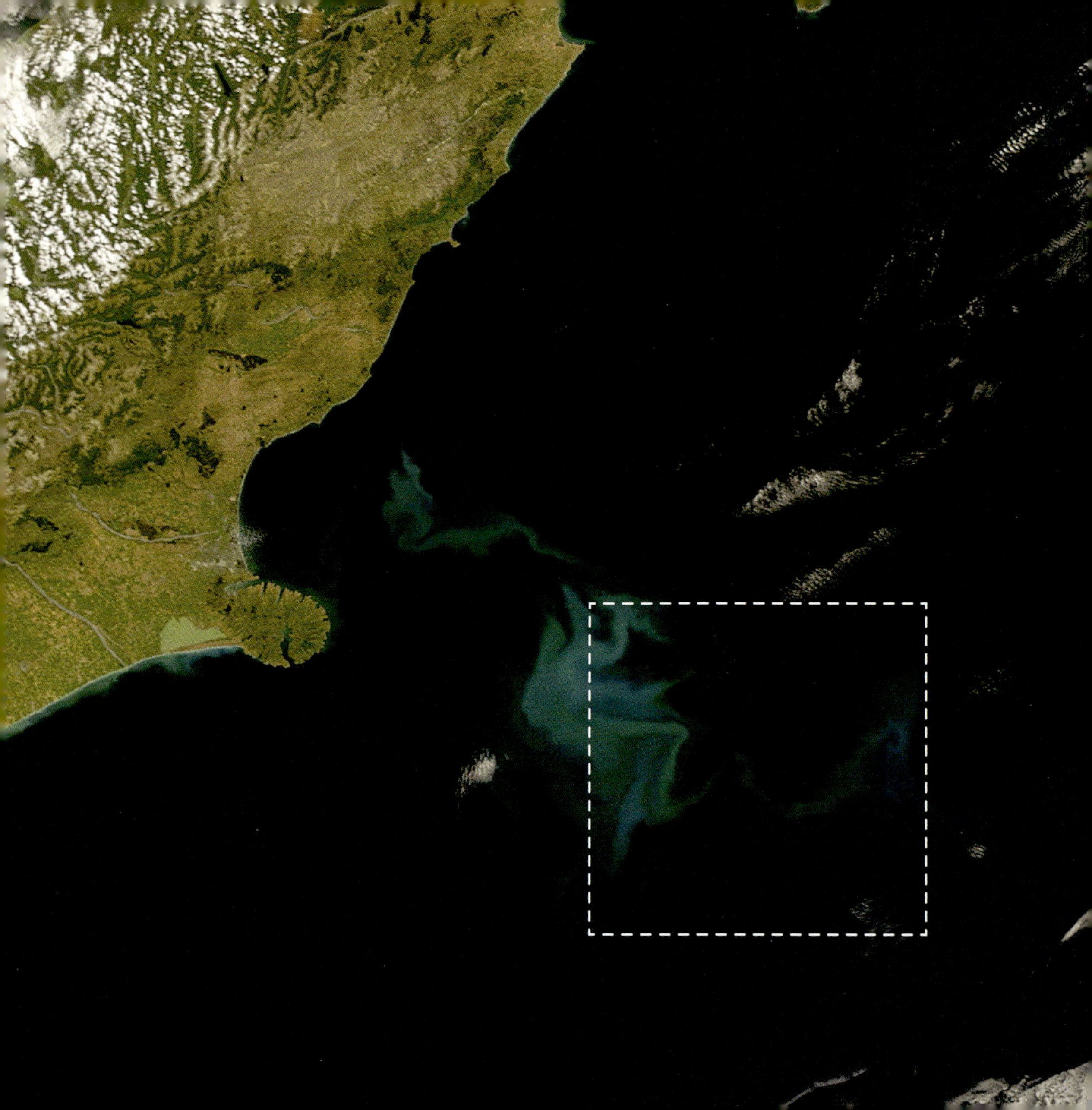

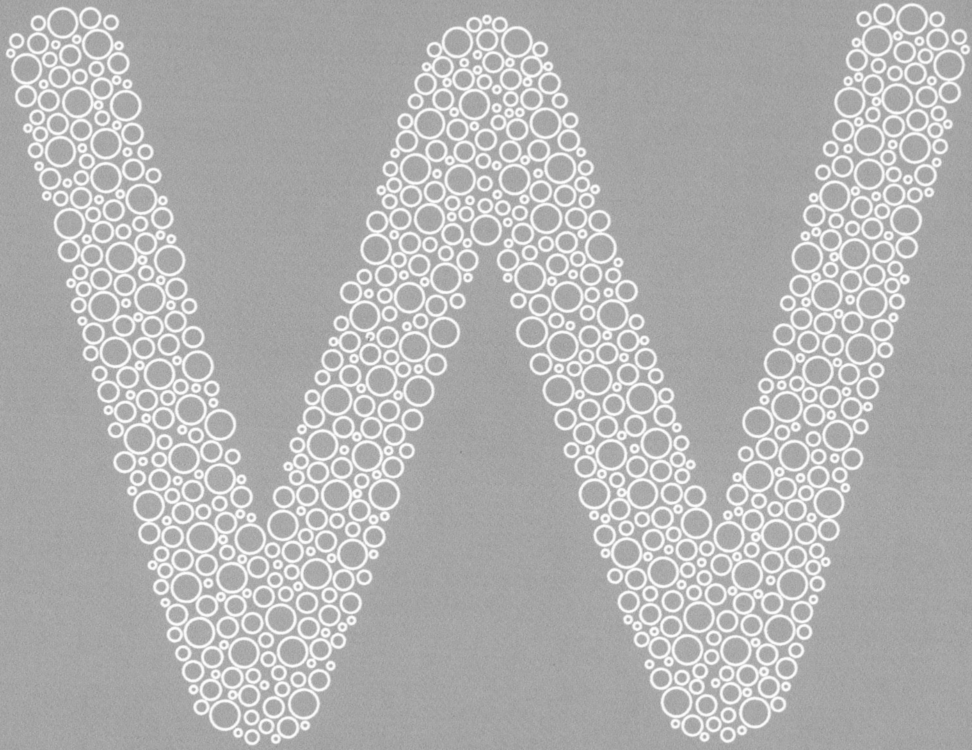

PHYTOPLANKTON BLOOM NEAR NEW ZEALAND

What's up, **W**? Water, wind and weather are W words.
So are Wales and Washington, D.C. And this wonderful whorl of **plankton** washing through wind-blown waters.

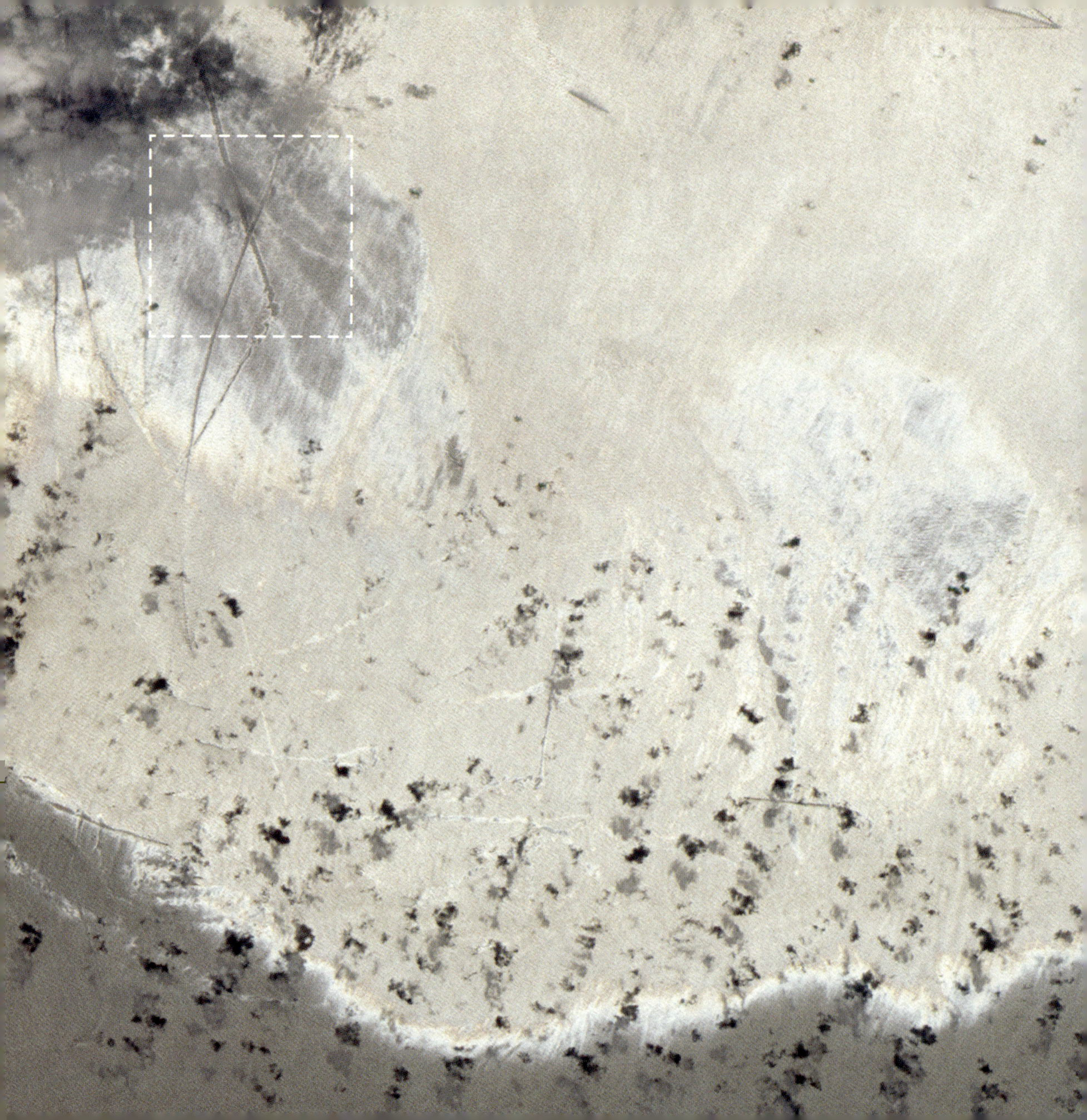

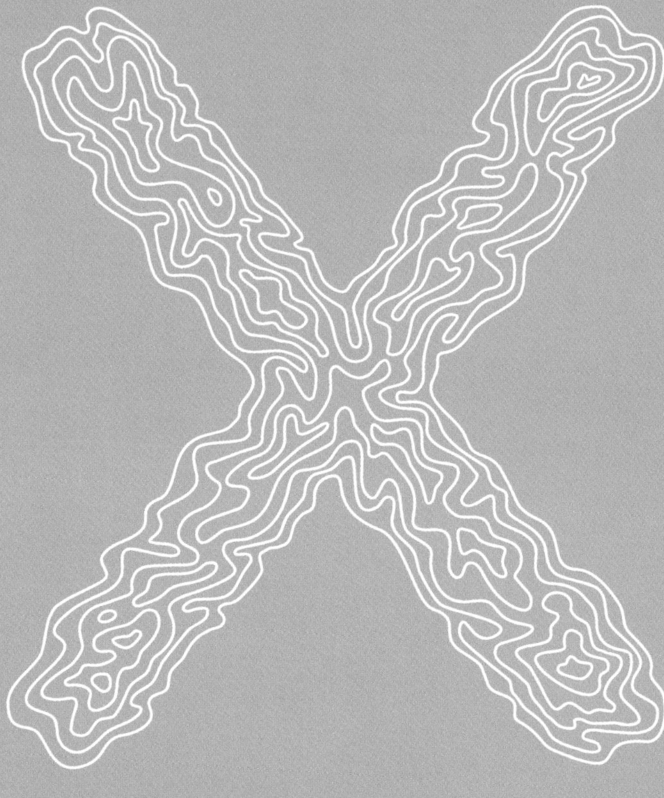

X, what begins with **X**? There are **xenoliths**, the **xylem** in **xeric** woodlands, and the cities of Xian and Xalapa. Not much else begins with X, so instead eXamine this eXceptionally noXious and toXic oil spill in the Gulf of MeXico.

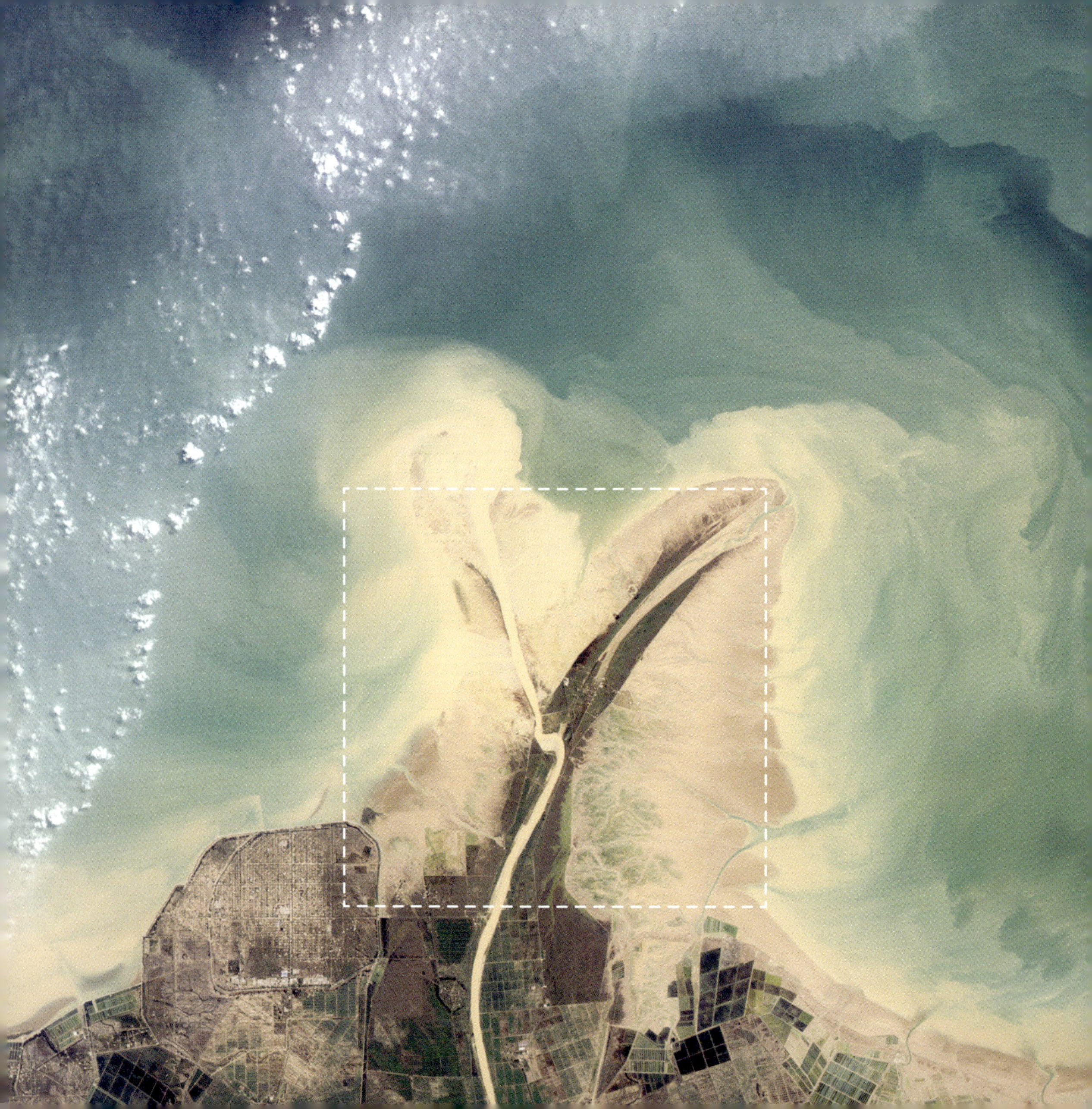

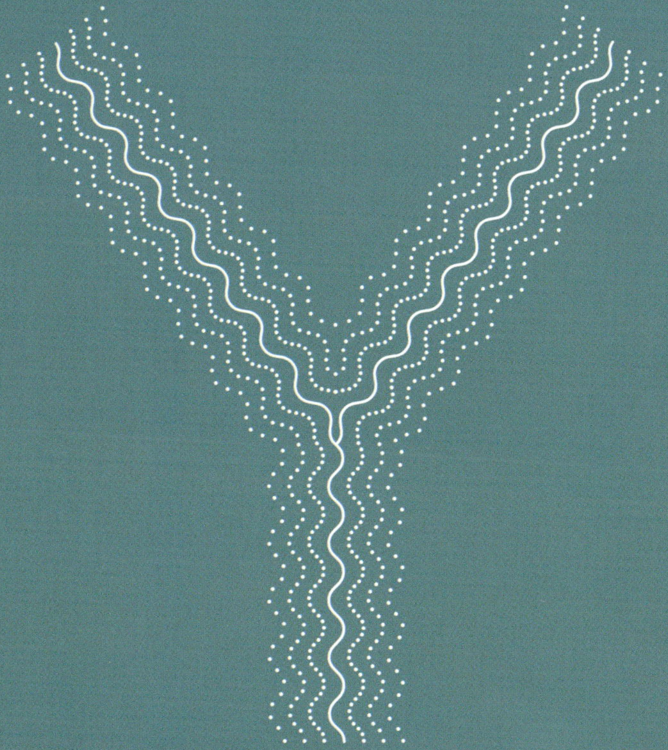

You there, **Y**. Yemen and York start with you. **Yardangs** and **yazoo streams**.
And this image – not of yaks doing yoga or a yard sale for yams –
of the muddy Yellow River flowing into the Pacific Ocean.

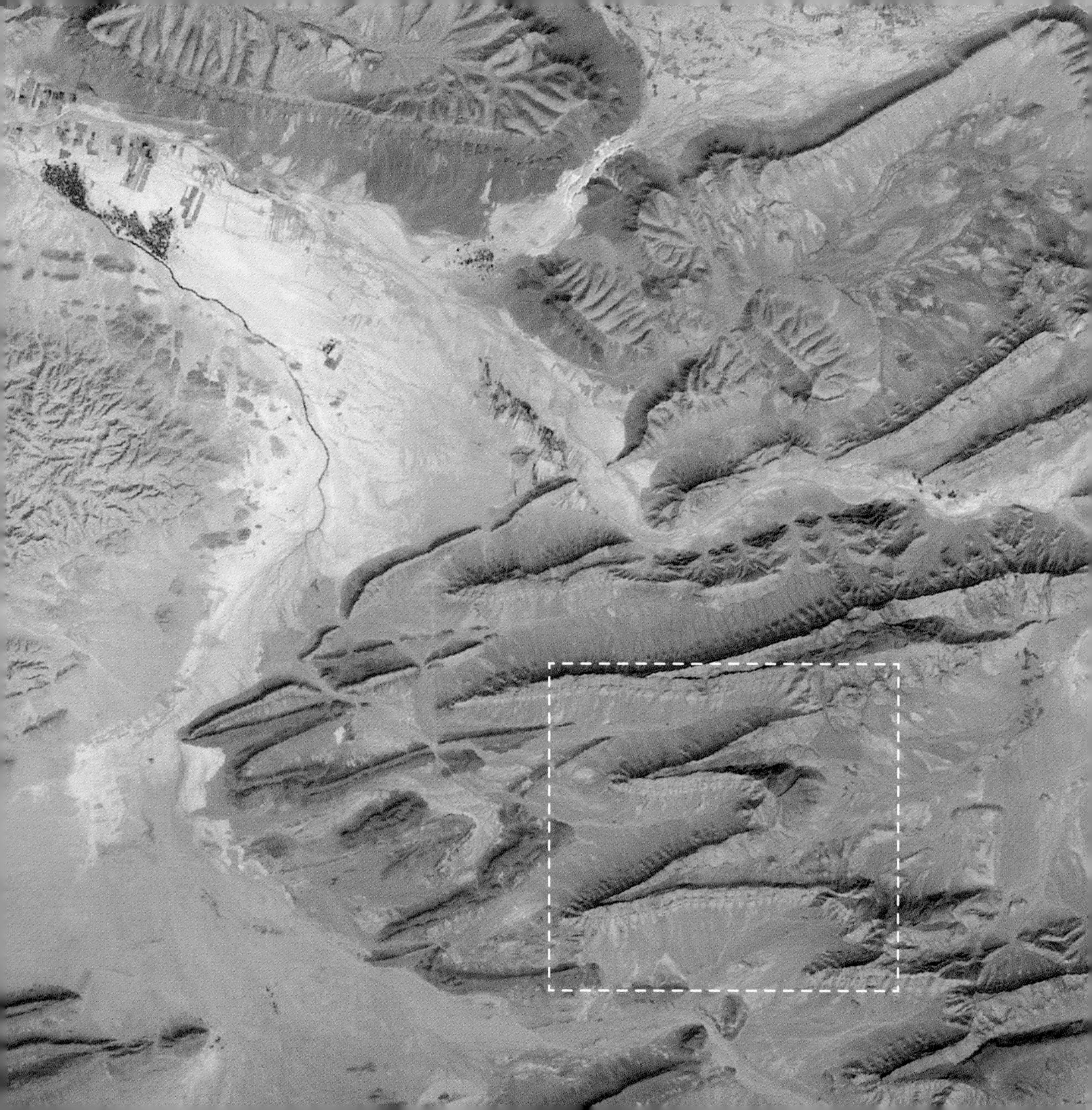

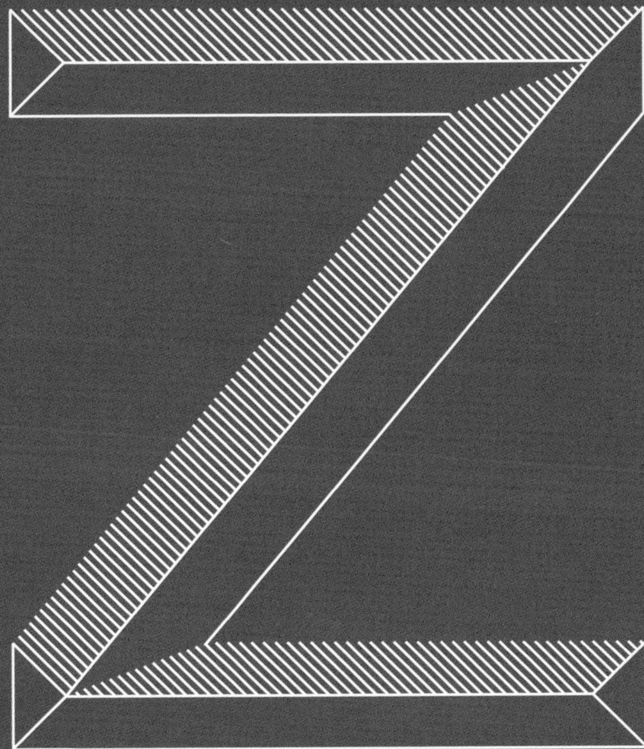

Zounds, there's **Z**! Zambia and Zimbabwe begin with Z. Zoology and **zircon**. And this zany zigzagging rock formation in a mountain range in Morocco.

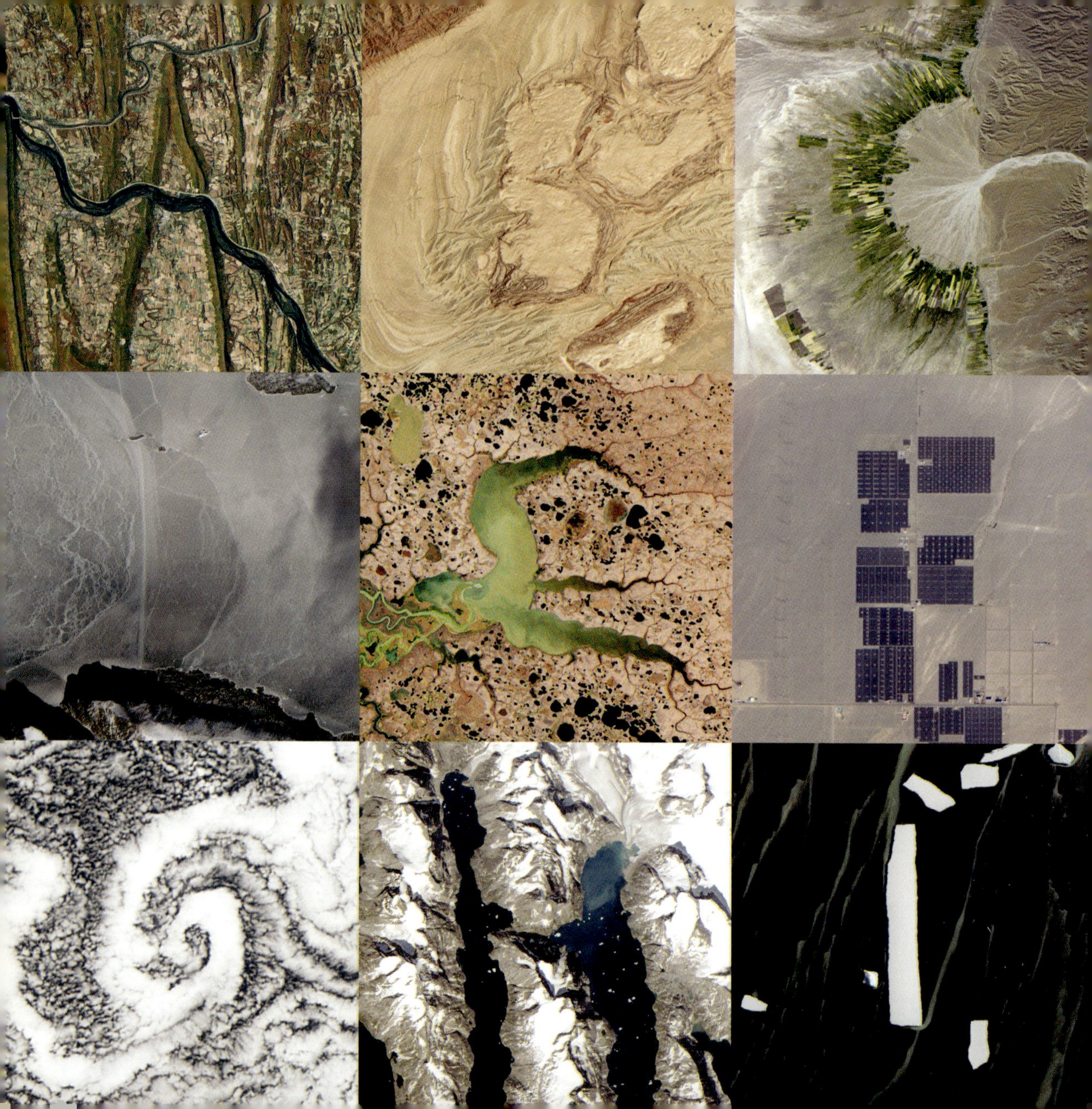

Appendix for Adults

A In central Pennsylvania, the Susquehanna River flows through five ridges of the Appalachian mountain range. Geologists think a network of **fractures** in the rock made these portions of the ridges more vulnerable to erosion. Notice how the river flows parallel to them for a distance before finding weak points. The **ETM+** sensor on the **Landsat 7 satellite** captured this image on 21 October 2001.

B The B-shaped rock formation in central Iran is the result of an underlying salt dome, a rising column of sodium chloride that was squeezed upward by the pressure of overlying rock layers. When salt domes break through to the surface and encounter water, they produce flowing structures called salt glaciers. The OLI sensor on the **Landsat 8 satellite** captured this image on 14 August 2015.

C **Alluvial fans** are triangular deposits of gravel, sand and silt. They form when streams flow from the sides of mountains, hills or other steep terrain into valleys where they break from their channels and fan out. In this dry part of Iran, the water often flows underground rather than at the surface. The **ASTER** sensor on the Terra **satellite** acquired this image on 12 October 2004.

D Situated well north of the Arctic Circle, Uummannaq island is home to one of the most northerly towns in Greenland. Winter brings months of darkness and a build-up of sea ice. Cracks often form in sea ice due to tides, shifting winds and currents. The ALI sensor on the **Earth Observing-1 satellite** acquired this image on 16 May 2012.

E **Deltas** form where streams and rivers drain into another body of water, often the sea. This image shows part of Alaska's Yukon River delta, one of the largest deltas in the world. The remote region has few roads; the best way to travel is by plane, boat or dog sled. The **ETM+** sensor on the **Landsat 7 satellite** acquired this image on 22 September 2002.

F For centuries, traders relied on an oasis in Dunhuang, China, for relief from the withering sunlight and heat of the Gobi desert. Now, a fast-expanding solar farm on the city's outskirts is converting that sunlight into electricity. The ALI sensor on the **Earth Observing-1** satellite captured this image of huge blocks of solar panels on 28 February 2016.

G Exhaust fumes from ship engines contain small particles that can serve as seeds for bright clouds called ship tracks. Water molecules cluster around the particles when pressure, temperature and humidity conditions are right. The cloud that makes up the G most likely achieved its spiral shape thanks to shifting winds and the ship's trajectory. The **MODIS** sensor on the Terra **satellite** captured this image of the north Pacific on 20 April 2013.

H The edges of the H are formed by parallel fjords in southeastern Greenland. Fjords are narrow water-filled valleys with steep sides. Most fjord valleys have broad U-shaped bottoms that were carved over time by **glaciers** grinding against the land surface. Fjords form when glaciers retreat and rising seas fill the valley floors. This image was captured by the **OLI** sensor on the **Landsat 8 satellite** on 8 August 2015.

I **Ice shelves** are floating sheets of thick ice connected to a land mass. The narrow iceberg that makes up the I broke off from the northwestern edge of Amery Ice Shelf in Antarctica's Mackenzie Bay. The blue-green patch below it is **frazil** ice – needle-like ice crystals suspended in water. Frazil is the first stage of sea ice growth. The ALI sensor on the **Earth Observing-1** satellite acquired this image on 12 February 2012.

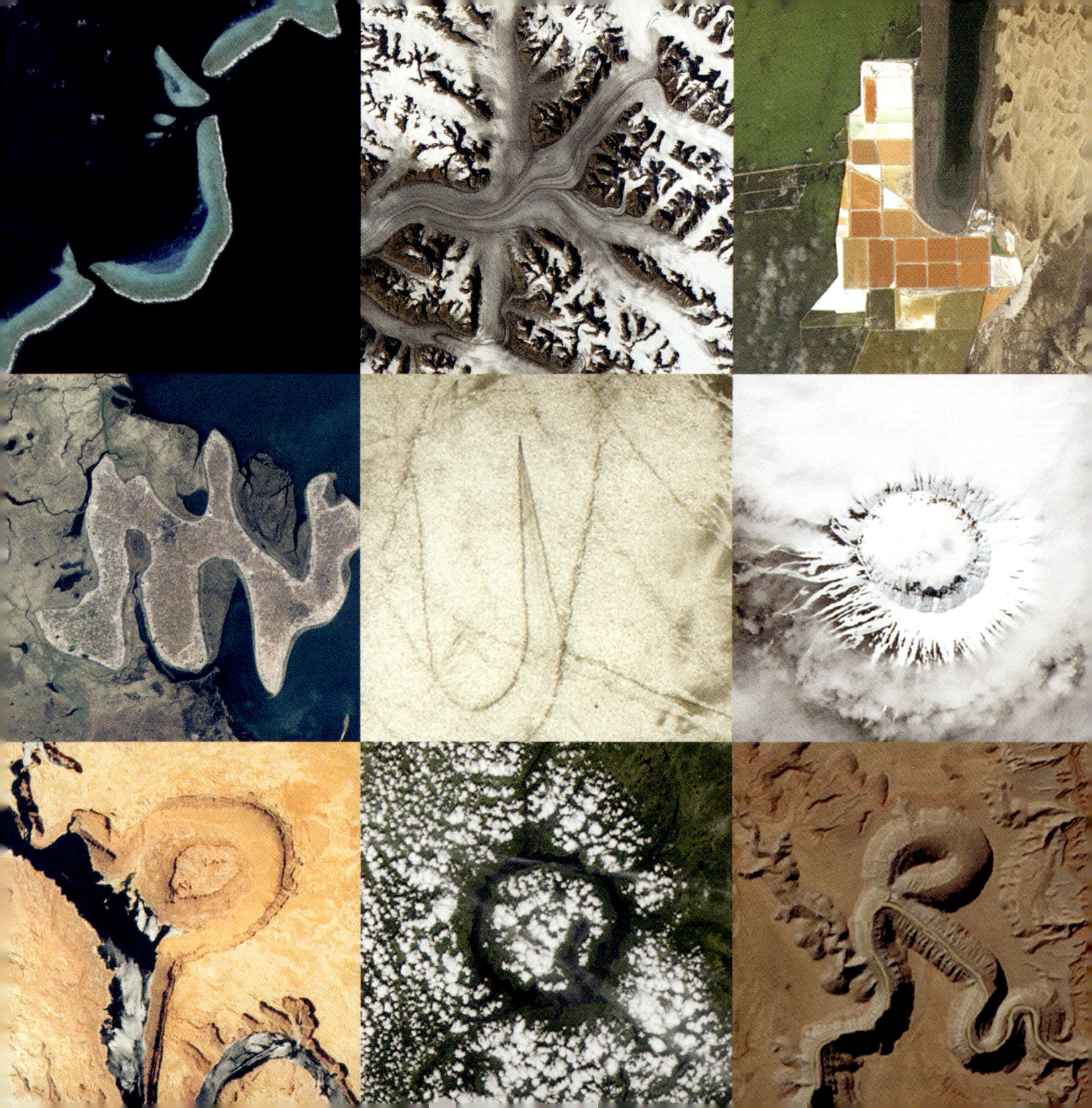

J Australia's Great Barrier Reef is the largest coral **reef** system in the world. Arrayed along the country's northeastern coast, it includes some 2,900 individual reefs and 900 islands. The J is formed by Bligh Reef, which is located east of the town of Lockhart in Queensland. The white line on the reef's eastern edge is caused by breaking waves. The **OLI** sensor on **Landsat 8** captured this image on 16 August 2015.

K **Glaciers** are akin to frozen rivers. They flow downstream and often curve as they navigate around obstacles. The glacier that makes up the K – Femstjernen in south-eastern Greenland — has several streams of ice flowing into it. The lines on the surface of the glaciers are medial moraines, soil and rock that builds up when glaciers merge. The **OLI** sensor on **Landsat 8** acquired this image on 17 August 2015.

L The orange salt evaporation ponds that make up the L are located in coastal Namibia near Walvis Bay. The shallow ponds are filled with seawater and produce salt as the water evaporates away. The water is orange because a particular type of algae thrives in the high-salinity environment. The ALI sensor on NASA's Earth **Observing-1 satellite** captured this image on 27 February 2011.

M This unusually shaped island in Zambia's Lake Bangweulu is mostly sand. Its coastlines, along with those of other nearby sand islands, have been smoothed by easterly winds. Aquatic vegetation is growing in the light-green areas surrounding the island. An astronaut aboard the **International Space Station** took this photograph using a Nikon D4 digital camera with a 1150-millimetre lens on 14 June 2015.

N **Sunglint** occurs when sunlight is reflected directly back at a camera or **satellite** sensor. The optical phenomenon transforms dark-blue water into an opaque silver or cream colour. In this case, the sunglint has illuminated the wakes of small boats on the surface of Lake Erie. An astronaut aboard the International Space Station took this photograph with a Kodak 760C digital camera using a 800-millimetre lens on 28 May 2006.

O Four distinctive mountains are clustered together in this part of the Aleutian island chain. Called Islands of Four Mountains, these peaks are the upper slopes of volcanoes that rise up from the sea floor. Herbert Island's **caldera** — a crater two kilometers wide — makes up the O. When the **OLI** sensor on **Landsat 8** captured this image on 8 June 2013, banks of clouds obscured all but the tops of the peaks.

P The loop that makes up the top of the P is an old **meander** in the Colorado River. The river stopped flowing through it several thousand years ago when it cut across the ends of the loop and shortened its course by several kilometres. An astronaut on the International Space Station took this photograph on 30 April 2012 using a Nikon D2Xs digital camera with a 400-millimetre lens.

Q Geologists believe Manicouagan **Crater** in Canada formed about 215 million years ago when an asteroid slammed into North America. One sign that the feature had otherworldly origins is the presence of **shocked quartz**, a mineral with a distinctive structure created by exposure to intense pressure. The **MODIS** sensor on the Terra **satellite** captured this image on 7 July 2009.

R The San Juan River sculpted these sinuous **canyons** in southern Utah. **Meandering** rivers are present all over the world, but not all of them carve deep canyons. In this case, the canyons grew especially deep because the entire land surface was slowly rising even as the river carved the channel downward. The **OLI** on **Landsat 8** acquired this image on 8 November 2015.

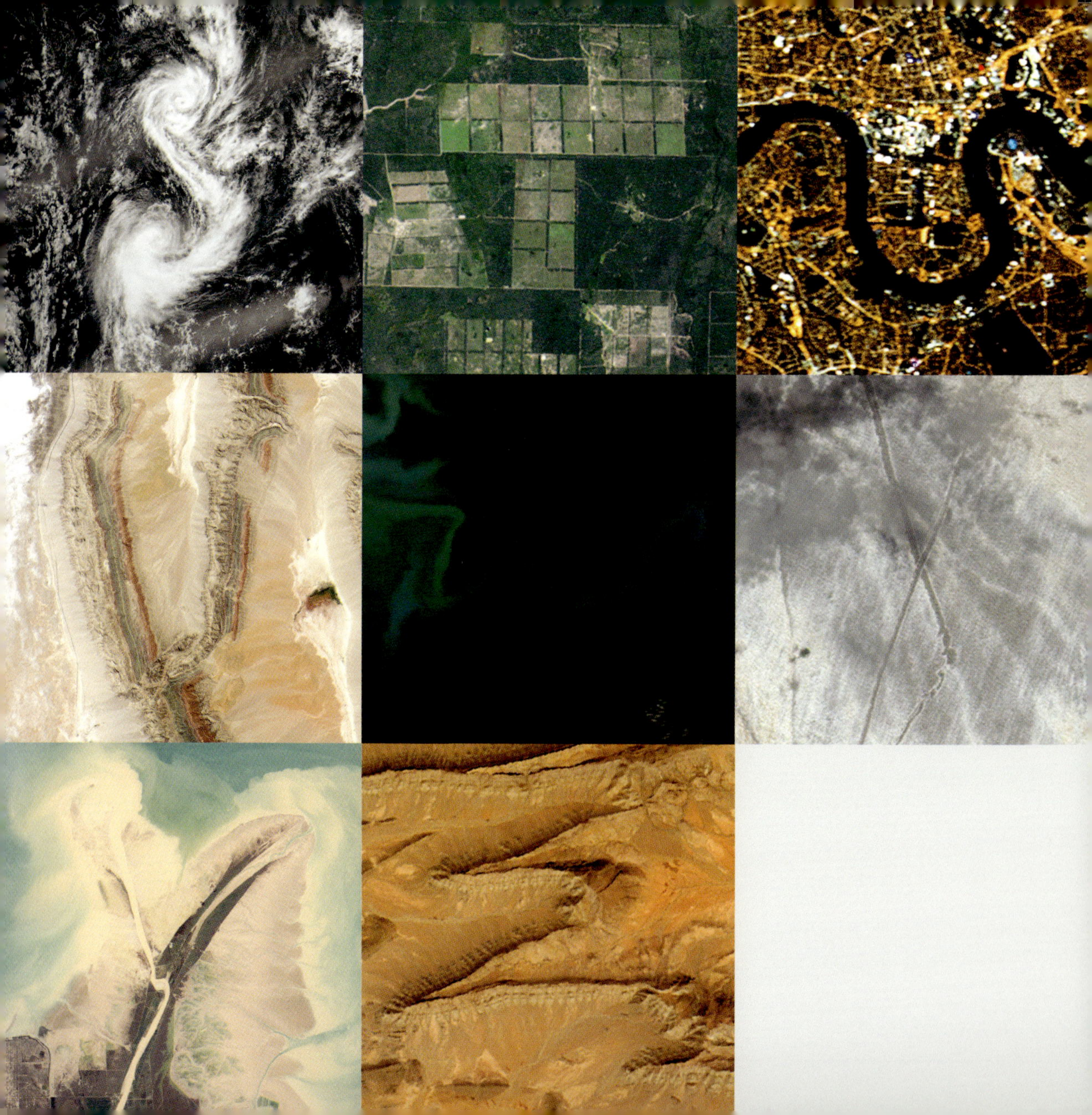

S Two tropical cyclones – named Diamondra and Eunice – swirled over the central Indian Ocean in January 2015. If two tropical cyclones are close enough, they can start to rotate around one another. Binary storm systems like this can even merge if their centres get close enough. The **VIIRS** sensor on the Suomi NPP satellite acquired this image of the twin storms on 28 January 2015.

T The dry forests of Paraguay, Argentina, Bolivia and Brazil are experiencing one of the fastest rates of **deforestation** in the world. Dark-green areas in this image are undisturbed forest; brown areas have been recently cleared, usually to establish pens for livestock or fields for soybeans. As vegetation regrows, cleared areas become light green. The **OLI** on **Landsat 8** acquired this image on 11 May 2010.

U Some of the city's most famous sites are visible in this night-time photograph of London. Look carefully, and you should be able to pick out Hyde Park and Tower Bridge amidst the city's lights. A **meander** in the River Thames, the second longest river in the United Kingdom, makes up the U. European Space Agency astronaut Tim Peake took this photograph using a Nikon D4 digital camera with a 400-millimetre lens on 27 September 2015.

V A range of environmental conditions created the series of colourful ridges that dominate this landscape in northwestern Xinjiang province in China. The red layers are sandstones formed by ancient rivers; the green layers are sandstones formed in a moderately deep ocean; the cream-coloured layers are **limestone** formed in a shallow ocean. The **OLI** on the **Landsat 8 satellite** captured this image on 30 July 2013.

W The blue swirls that make up the W are caused by a bloom of phyto**plankton**. Phytoplankton are tiny ocean-dwelling organisms that thrive in cool waters near the ocean surface that are rich in nutrients. Wind tends to be good for phytoplankton because it makes water more turbulent and brings nutrients to the surface. The **MODIS** sensor on NASA's Terra **satellite** captured this image on 5 January 2008.

X The Deepwater Horizon oil spill is the largest marine oil spill in history. Oil gushed unchecked from an underwater well off the coast of Louisiana for more than two months. In this image, the X is formed by boat wakes cutting through the sheen of the oil. The mirror-like reflection of **sunglint** makes oil spills more noticeable in satellite imagery. The ALI sensor on the **Earth Observing-1 satellite** captured this image on 21 May 2010.

Y The Yellow River once deposited massive amounts of sediment – mud, sand and silt – at the Yellow River **delta** in China. However, sediment loads have declined more than 90 per cent over the last 60 years because of the construction of dams and reservoirs and the increased use of terracing by farmers. The Thematic Mapper on the **Landsat 5 satellite** captured this image on 20 June 2009.

Z The sharply folded ridges that makes up the Z lie in the Anti-Atlas mountain range in southwestern Morocco. After continental collisions built the mountains, they eroded away at different rates based on the toughness of the exposed rocks. For instance, shale wears away more easily than sandstone. The **ETM+** sensor on the **Landsat 7 satellite** captured this image on 19 March 2002.

Glossary for Geography Geeks

algal bloom: a sudden spurt of algae growth spurred by an influx of nutrients.

alluvial fans: triangle-shaped deposits of gravel, sand and silt; they form when streams flowing down slopes fan out in valley floors.

Advanced Spaceborne Thermal Emission and Reflection Radiometer (ASTER): a multi-spectral sensor on NASA's Terra satellite with a maximum resolution of 15 metres per pixel.

Big Bang: the rapid expansion of matter from a state of extremely high density and temperature. Marked the origin of the universe, according to current theory.

caldera: a large volcanic crater caused by the collapse of the land surface into an empty magma chamber.

canyon: a deep gorge, typically one with a river flowing through it.

crater: a large, bowl-shaped cavity in the ground.

deforestation: the clearing of trees by fire, saw, or other means.

delta: a landform that forms from deposition of sediment carried by a river as the flow leaves its mouth and enters slower-moving or standing water.

Earth Observing-1: an experimental Earth-observing spacecraft launched by NASA in 2000.

eclipse: temporary blocking of the light from one celestial body by the passage of another between it and the observer or between it and its source of illumination.

Einstein: German-born physicist famous for developing the general theory of relativity.

Enhanced Thematic Mapper Plus (ETM+): a multi-spectral imager on Landsat 7 with a maximum resolution of 15 metres per pixel.

equator: an imaginary line around Earth that is equally distant from both poles and divides the planet into northern and southern hemispheres.

estuary: the transition zone between freshwater rivers and oceans.

fossils: hardened remains of plant or animal life from a previous geological period preserved in the Earth's crust.

fractures: a fracture is any separation in a rock formation.

frazil: small needle-like ice crystals suspended in water; the first stage of sea ice growth.

frost: a deposit of small white ice crystals formed on the ground or other surfaces when the temperature falls below freezing.

glacier: a mass of land ice that flows continuously from higher to lower elevations.

global warming: an increase in the near-surface temperature of Earth.

greenhouse gas: gases such as carbon dioxide, methane, nitrous oxide, chlorofluorocarbons, and water vapour that can trap heat in Earth's atmosphere.

haze: fine dry or wet particles of dust, salt or other impurities suspended in the air that reduce visibility by scattering light.

horizon: the horizon is the apparent line that separates earth from sky.

hydrology: the scientific study of water on Earth.

ice shelf: ice shelves are permanent floating sheets of ice that connect to a landmass; mostly found in Antarctica.

International Space Station: a habitable space laboratory built by five countries that orbits Earth at an average altitude of 400 kilometres above the surface.

isthmus: a narrow strip of land with sea on either side, forming a link between two larger areas of land.

jet stream: rivers of high-speed air in the atmosphere that form along boundaries of global air masses with differing temperatures.

Johnson Space Center: the NASA centre where astronauts are stationed and trained; location of 'Mission Control' for many high-profile NASA programmes.

katabatic wind: a wind that carries high-density air from a higher elevation down a slope due to the force of gravity.

kelp: a large brown seaweed.

kettle ponds: shallow bodies of water that are sculpted by retreating glaciers. Kettles form when blocks of ice break from glaciers, became submerged in soil and eventually melt.

Landsat programme: the longest-running series of satellites acquiring imagery of Earth; the first Landsat satellite was launched in 1972.

lava lake: lava lakes are large volumes of molten lava, usually contained in a volcanic vent or crater.

limestone: a sedimentary rock composed mainly of calcium carbonate; sometimes composed of the remains (shells and corals) of marine organisms.

magma: a very hot molten and semi-molten rock mixture found under the surface.

mammatus clouds: a cellular pattern of pouches hanging underneath the base of certain cumulus clouds.

meander: a bend in a sinuous watercourse or river.

meteor: a piece of rock or metal that burns and glows brightly in the sky as it falls from outer space into the Earth's atmosphere.

Moderate Resolution Imaging Spectroradiometer (MODIS):
a multispectral imager on NASA's Terra and Aqua satellites with a maximum resolution of 250 metres per pixel.

Newton: an English physicist and mathematician who formulated the laws of motion and universal gravitation; he built the first reflecting telescope.

ooids: small oval-shaped spheres of mainly calcium carbonate.

Operational Land Imager (OLI): a multi-spectral imager on the Landsat 8 satellite with a maximum resolution of 15 metres per pixel.

pancake ice: pancake ice is a form of ice that has round pieces of ice with diameters ranging from 30 centimetres to 3 metres.

plankton: the small and microscopic organisms drifting or floating in the sea or fresh water.

plateau: an area of relatively level high ground.

quantum theory: a theory in physics based on the concept that energy (for instance, light) is made of small separate units of energy.

Quaternary period: a geological time period that encompasses the most recent 2.6 million years – including the present day.

radar: an object-detection system that uses radio waves to determine the range, angle or velocity of objects.

rainforest: an evergreen woodland of the tropics characterized by a continuous leaf canopy and an average rainfall of about 254 centimetres per year.

reef: a ridge of jagged rock, coral or sand just above or below the surface of the sea.

satellites: a free-flying object that orbits the Earth, another planet, or the Sun.

savanna: an environment defined by extensive grass cover with scattered trees.

shocked quartz: a structurally altered form of quartz created by a sudden pulse of extremely high pressure. Found in meteorite impact craters and nuclear bomb explosions.

sunglint: a phenomenon that occurs when sunlight reflects off the surface of the ocean at the same angle that a satellite or other sensor is viewing the surface.

typhoon: a cyclonic storm similar to a hurricane that occurs in the Indian or western Pacific oceans.

undertow: a current in the ocean that is below the surface and that moves away from the shore

upwelling: a process in which deep, cold water rises towards the surface.

Visible Infrared Imaging Radiometer Suite (VIIRS): a multispectral imager on the Suomi NPP satellite with a maximum resolution of 375 metres per pixel.

vog: smog or haze containing volcanic dust and gases.

volcano: a break in the crust that allows hot lava, volcanic ash and gases to escape from a magma chamber below the surface.

xenolith: a piece of rock trapped in another type of rock.

xeric: an environment with minimal moisture.

xylem: a type of tissue in plants that transports water.

yazoo stream: a tributary that parallels the main channel of a stream for a considerable distance.

yardangs: streamlined rock formations found in deserts sculpted by winds.

zircon: a type of mineral; zircon from Australia has been shown to be 4.4 billion years old, making it the oldest known mineral in the world.

Acknowledgements & Credits

This book would not have been possible without the help and support of many others.

Thank you to Michael Carlowicz for nearly eight years of steady and thoughtful editing. Thank you to Kevin Ward and the rest of the NASA Earth Observatory team both past and present – particularly Robert Simmon, Paul Przyborski, Joshua Stevens, Holli Riebeek, Michon Scott, Kathyrn Hansen and Jesse Allen (again) – for offering invaluable insights about how to interpret satellite imagery over the years. Thank you to Piers Sellers for your leadership, courage and commitment to the planet. Thank you to Charles Ichoku, Claire Parkinson, Paul Newman, Ralph Kahn and many other scientists at NASA's Goddard Space Flight Center and elsewhere who regularly take time from their busy schedules to fact-check my writing and to answer my questions about all aspects of earth science.

Thank you to the NASA Crew Earth Observations office and the MODIS, LANDSAT, VIIRS and ASTER science teams. Without the efforts of those groups, there would be no imagery for this book.

Thank you especially to Jeff Schmaltz for teaching me so much about MODIS. Thank you to Win Decker, Anoop Mehta and the rest of the broader Science Systems and Applications, Inc. (SSAI) team for their unwavering support of this project.

Thank you to Katy Follain and the rest of the team at Quercus for her vision, her thoughtful editing and her enthusiasm for this book. I still can't quite believe we made the Father's Day deadline. Thank you to Sarah Greeno for the spectacular illustrations and beautiful design. And thank you to Farley Chase of Chase Literary Agency for patiently guiding me through the details of what it takes to pull a book together.

Finally, thank you, Dad, for always reminding me to look for wonder and beauty in the natural world. Thank you, Mom, for always listening to all of my moaning about deadlines. Most important of all, thank you, Katherine, for your incredible understanding and patience about all those times I had to lock myself away to search for letters or to work on a story. I love you all so much.

A NASA/USGS/Landsat 7/ETM+
B NASA/USGS/Landsat 8/OLI
C NASA/JAXA/Terra/ASTER
D NASA/USGS/Earth Observing-1/ALI
E NASA/USGS/Landsat 7/ETM+
F NASA/USGS/Earth Observing-1/ALI
G NASA/Terra/MODIS
H NASA/USGS/Landsat 8/OLI
I NASA/USGS/Earth Observing-1/ALI
J NASA/USGS/Landsat 8/OLI
K NASA/USGS/Landsat 8/OLI
L NASA/USGS/Earth Observing-1/ALI
M NASA/ISS/Astronaut photograph
N NASA/ISS/Astronaut photograph
O NASA/USGS/Landsat 8/OLI
P NASA/ISS/Astronaut photograph
Q NASA/Terra/MODIS
R NASA/USGS/Landsat 8/OLI
S NASA/NOAA/Suomi NPP/VIIRS
T NASA/USGS/Landsat 8/OLI
U NASA/ISS/Astronaut photograph
V NASA/USGS/Landsat 8/OLI
W NASA/Terra/MODIS
X NASA/USGS/Landsat 8/ALI
Y NASA/USGS/Landsat 5/TM
Z NASA/USGS/Landsat 7/ETM+